An Introduction to Bus. ... ETHICS

Introducing Philosophy

Introducing Philosophy is a series of textbooks designed to introduce the basic topics of philosophy for any student approaching the subject for the first time. Each volume presents a central subject of philosophy by considering the key issues and outlooks associated with the area. With the emphasis firmly on the arguments for and against a philosophical position, the reader is encouraged to think philosophically about the subject.

An Introduction to Business Ethics

Jennifer Jackson

The right of Jennifer Jackson to be identified as author of this work has been asserted in accordance with the Copyright, Designs and Patents Act 1988.

First published 1996

2 4 6 8 10 9 7 5 3 1

Blackwell Publishers Ltd
108 Cowley Road
Oxford OX4 1JF
UK

Blackwell Publishers Inc.
238 Main Street
Cambridge, Massachusetts 02142
USA

British Library Cataloguing in Publication Data

A CIP catalogue record for this book is available from the British Library.

Library of Congress Cataloging-in-Publication Data

Jackson, Jennifer C., 1939–
      An introduction to business ethics / Jennifer Jackson.
         p.   cm. — (Introducing philosophy)
      Includes bibliographical references and index.
      ISBN 0–631–19532–7 (hbk. : alk. paper). — ISBN 0–631–19533–5
   (pbk. : alk. paper)
      1. Business ethics.   I. Title.   II. Series.
   HF5387.J295   1996
   174′.4—dc20
                                                              96–11696
                                                                   CIP

Typeset in 11 on 13 pt Bembo
by Graphicraft Typesetters Ltd, Hong Kong
Printed in Great Britain by Hartnolls Ltd, Bodmin, Cornwall

This book is printed on acid-free paper

Contents

Acknowledgements

I am grateful to the many people who have helped me towards the writing of this book. The initial planning and research was undertaken with the support of a Tennent Caledonian Visiting Research Fellowship at the Centre for Philosophy and Public Affairs at the University of St. Andrews in the authumn term of 1992. I gratefully acknowledge this financial support, and the friendly encouragement and stimulating academic environment provided in the Centre. I owe a continuing debt to my students and to my colleagues, academic and administrative, including some now retired, in the Philosophy Department at the University of Leeds, who have made my teaching and studying here so enjoyable. Particular thanks are owed to two of my colleagues, Christopher Coope and Chris Megone, who bore the main burden of my departmental responsibilities while I was at St. Andrews. Professor David Holdcroft read and made helpful comments on a large chunk of my manuscript. Christopher Coope made detailed comment on the whole of it, guiding me to much needed revision, editing and clarification. I also benefited greatly from the comments of the Blackwell readers. A special thanks to the editor, Nathalie Manners, for her patience and encouragement throughout. Finally, my greatest debt is to my family, children and spouse, for their good-humoured endurance of my preoccupation with this work.

Introduction

By 'business ethics' let us understand: the study of practices and policies in business, to determine which are ethically defensible and which are not. The purpose of this book is to explain why people in business need to join in this study and to suggest how they should set about it, what they can expect to get out of it and what they should be able to give to it. In order to make good my claim that it is worth while for business people to engage in this study, I have to show that business people need to take part – they have something to learn that they do not know already and that they need to know. This book aims to be relevantly informative – to help people in business to find their way in dealing with the ethical problems that they can expect to face and do need help with.

Is this a credible aim? Let us consider two kinds of doubt: the first about the feasibility of studying ethics in order to determine what practices are ethically defensible – as against what practices are thought to be so – and the second about the usefulness to people in business of the results of such a study even if it is feasible and ably conducted.

The Feasibility of Practical Ethics

Practical ethics (or practical morality – I will use the terms interchangeably), let us understand to be about 'how we should live with each other and with ourselves'. But is this something that it makes sense to study? Some people are so struck by the difficulty of reconciling differences of view on moral matters, especially between people from different cultures, that they adopt a position of moral relativism: they contend that there are no moral truths to be discovered; no such thing as *the* difference between right and wrong but simply the difference as drawn by this society or that. Thus, according to this relativist view, there can be no *critical* enquiry into what we *should* think is ethically defensible, only empirical enquiry into what we, or others, *do* happen to think.

But why should we agree with this view? There is no good reason to believe it and plenty of reasons to disbelieve it. There is no good reason to believe it: the mere fact that there is disagreement, even deep disagreement, on moral matters between different cultures is consistent with the truth of relativism but also with its falsity. There are plenty of reasons to disbelieve it, since if it were true we would have to abandon many of our convictions, such as, for example, the ideas that there can be moral progress – and regress – and that some practices accepted in other societies and not our own are less – or more – enlightened than our own. Part of the appeal of the relativist stance is that it cuts the ground from under the feet of those who adopt attitudes of moral superiority towards people of different cultures and customs. Yet just because we reject the relativist view about the impossibility of comparing customs and practices critically, we need not condone ignorant smugness and prejudice towards other people's strange customs.

In this book I proceed on the assumption that *critical* enquiry into what practices are and are not ethically defensible is feasible. We have enough in common with one another – in what we need, in what we are capable of, in our shared circumstances – that it is possible to speak *generally* about how we should live our lives, whoever 'we' are. In so saying, I make certain assumptions about what makes for living well and for living wretchedly and about the extent to which our individual fortunes depend on our *own* choices and attitudes. I assume that there are certain evils which can spoil *any* life – for example, loneliness, enslavement, poverty, boredom, lack of self-respect – and that to some extent it is in an individual's power to develop character traits that give one the best chance of avoiding the evils or, where that is not possible, minimizing the harm they do. These character traits we call 'moral virtues'.

How we fare in life depends plainly in many respects on factors beyond our own control – the times we live in, our own genetic inheritance, the kind of family, if any, we are born into, the opportunities that come our way through life, the accidents that befall us and those dear to us. Yet, however our personal histories unfold, the only influence or power we each of us can bring to bear on our fortunes is through developing virtues and avoiding vices. We do, of course, also influence our own fortunes through the skills we learn, the knowledge we acquire. But the powers we gain thereby only improve our lot in so far as we use judgement in how we apply them – for which we need virtues, as I shall argue. Individuals who are trustworthy, fair, courageous, wise, humane and industrious fare better in the hurly-burly of day to day living than do those who are shiftless, sneaky, cowardly, foolish, mean or lazy. This is true whether the individuals we are speaking of happen to be male or female, young or old, rich or poor, in robust health or invalids, Britons living in the 1990s or those to whom Aristotle gave his lectures on moral virtues in the Lyceum around 347 BC.

Consider, for example, the story in *A Suitable Boy* of how Haresh manages to double the production of shoes in Praha, a Czech footwear company located in India.[1] His business success, how he wins 'the Battle of Goodyear Welted', depends entirely on the impact of his character both on those under him and those over him in the managerial hierarchy. He wins the trust of those he has to persuade to cooperate by demonstrating not only his first-hand understanding of the work he is asking of them, but also his energy and perseverance, for he amazes the workers by himself accomplishing the task before their eyes that *they* say cannot be done. In similar style he astonishes his superiors. His transparent honesty and fairness coax the workers out of their habitual defensive practices. They are prepared to cooperate because they have reason to believe that it will be in their interests to succeed. They believe in him because he explains to them what he wants, how they can bring it about and why they will gain thereby. He takes them into his confidence as equals and they are won over.

No less impressive is how he overcomes the coolness of his Czech employers and their general prejudice against Indian employees. It is the same evident honesty, fairness, straight dealing, energy and informedness that wins them round. His virtues of character enable him to judge astutely what he and those with whom he deals are capable of, and what persuasions will be effective. The inspiration of his strategy and the shrewdness with which he brings it off are part and parcel of his moral character.

We can understand Haresh's success in the Praha company as a triumph of character, of his personal virtues. The story of his success is entirely credible because his virtues are recognizable to us – as to those with whom he deals – despite our own remoteness from the context in which these are demonstrated.

To be sure, establishing that fairness or honesty is a virtue does not of itself tell us what actions or choices are ethically defensible or indefensible. But it is a beginning towards answering that kind of question. It at least helps us to understand the importance of the study of ethics – we all of us want our lives to go as well as possible and to use what control we have over our own fates effectively: "t is in ourselves that we are thus, or thus. Our bodies are our gardens, to the which our wills are gardeners: so that if we will plant nettles, or sow lettuce; set hyssop, and weed up thyme; . . . why, the power and corrigible authority of this lies in our wills.'[2]

The Usefulness of Practical Ethics

Even if the aim of this book, to help people in business to find their way in dealing with ethical problems, is an intelligible one in that there are correct and incorrect answers to these problems, it may still be doubted whether a book of this nature is going to be useful to people in business. Those who care, who have a conscience, do not need instruction on business ethics, and those who don't care, aren't interested – it will be said.

But this is over-simple. Those who care are likely to be aware of how morally complex many decisions they have to make are. You may be appalled to think of young Indian children toiling through the day manufacturing cheap products that you stock in your shops. But if you cease to import their products do you in any way improve their chances of an education? What is *your* responsibility? Are they being exploited? If they are, are you implicated if you provide a market for their products? To take another case: you might have some information that is suggestive, but far from conclusive, that there is a link between incidents of leukaemia and the proximity to people's houses of power cables that you are having erected. The law, let us suppose, does not oblige you to bury cables – which would be extremely expensive – but should your conscience oblige you to do so?

Now, in order to deal with real problems in business where what is ethically defensible in the circumstances is not obvious even to those who *want* to act well, it helps to have an understanding of the basic moral notions. Perhaps many people have this understanding although they do not, and maybe could not, if called upon, articulate it. In order to convince others who do not agree with us as to what is ethically defensible or indefensible in a particular situation, it is necessary not only to understand but to be able to explain. In order ourselves to resolve ethical problems even to our own satisfaction, we need to develop the vocabulary in which to meditate on them. My aim is to provide explanation, to provide a philosophical backbone for business ethics. It is easy to underestimate the importance of introducing the study of business ethics with an analysis of certain basic notions – notions of right and wrong, good and bad, obligation and virtues. Perhaps just because these are all very familiar notions, not in any way technical, we assume that our understanding of them is adequate and that we do not need to reflect on their meaning. We do. Many introductions to this or that branch of practical ethics breeze too lightly over this necessary preliminary to the study of cases. It pays to take our first steps with great care, rather than to hurry down any path that beckons. The philosophical backbone is needed to give us a firm basis for addressing the practical issues.

This book does not tell people in business what is ethically defensible or indefensible where that is not already obvious to honest, reasonable people. What it offers, though, is information that such people themselves need to understand if they are to work out the substantive answers in morally complex situations. I offer a map of morality and the marching orders for anyone in business (whether doing business just on one's own behalf, on behalf of a commercial enterprise or on behalf of a charity). The map will be of no use to people in business who think they know the way and need no guidance for dealing with the ethical dimension to the decisions they make. But for those who feel the need, the map should help them to a basic understanding of the complexities of choice, of what makes choices difficult and why it matters how one chooses, and of what more needs to be done with the basic map so as to make it more informative in this or that line of business. My aim is to set people on the right track, not to lead them along it. In short, this book is strictly an introduction to business ethics – but one that aims to make the reader glad to have been introduced.

Business ethics, I maintain, requires both philosophy to provide a basic map of morality and the judgement of people experienced in a business to fill in the detail on the basic map. The basic map has to do with what Elaine Sternberg calls 'the eternal verities'[3] – it should not change over time, although there may be superficial updatings of presentation to make it accessible to different audiences. The filling in of details on the map, though, will vary depending not just on whether those who are adding detail are improving the map for their business colleagues as against doing so for nursing or teaching colleagues, but depending on the specific type of business, the scale, the society in which it operates, the level of technology involved and many other variables. The basic map calls for philosophical understanding, the more detailed map calls for experience-based knowledge within a particular business. But those who provide the detail need first to get hold of the basic map and then to understand it. This is what I hope to explain in what follows.

Further Reading

On moral relativism
See Stace, 'Ethical relativity and ethical absolutism'; Sumner, 'A defense of cultural relativism'; Benedict, 'A defense of moral relativism'; Hospers, 'The problem with relativism'; Midgley, 'Trying out one's new sword'; Rachels, 'Egoism and moral scepticism'; Wong, 'Relativism'.

Study Questions

1 What else (other than the truth of moral relativism) might account for the difficulty of resolving disagreements on ethical issues?
2 Are there some ethical issues about which agreeing to disagree is ethically defensible and some about which doing so is not? Give examples of differences that you consider fellow members of a firm should/should not be prepared to tolerate. How do you decide what should/should not be tolerated?

1
Where to Begin

Two Kinds of Difficulty

There are two kinds of difficulty in ethics: difficulties in identification – of what is your duty in a particular situation, for
example; and difficulties of compliance – of doing your duty once
you know what it is. Perhaps the public's perception of business
ethics reflects its awareness of the latter (compliance) problem –
how to prevent skulduggery, mischief and negligence – whereas
the concerns of those people in business who recognize the
importance and relevance of business ethics reflects their awareness too of the former (identification) problem: how to establish
what policy or decision is fair and reasonable.

Identification Problems

What gives rise to identification problems, that is, problems over
what in particular circumstances it is ethically defensible to do?
One common kind of difficulty occurs where your role (or roles)
gives rise to competing claims tugging you to act in incompatible
ways, as when the obligation to be honest requires action that
injures the interests of those whom you have a duty to protect.
Suppose, for example, you are asked to report on the viability of
a branch of your firm: your honest and considered opinion may
be that the branch is not viable and that it is in the long-term
interests of the firm to close it down despite the valiant efforts
you know the employees there have dedicated to improving its

performance. On the other hand, in giving such advice are you not betraying the trust of those very employees who formerly rallied to your pleas for greater productivity and who are in no way to blame for the plant's present failures – their efforts are perhaps being undercut by foreign competition? Would these employees have stayed with the firm if they had not believed that you were advising them in their interests (as maybe you thought then you were doing)? Even if legally they have no claim against you, even if you did not make any explicit promise that the plant would be kept open, do they not have a moral claim on you – especially where you know that their prospects of finding other employment are now bleak?

Two things are worth noting about this kind of problem. Firstly, *that* you see the situation as ethically difficult does not show that there must be a deficiency in your moral character or moral education. On the contrary, those who are well-meaning, conscientious and thoughtful are more likely to be troubled about such situations than those who are not. Secondly, working out what it is right or all right to do in the particular case is not *just* a matter of having good guidelines, a well thought out code. However good the code, the problem of applying it in the particular case often requires judgement and study of all relevant particulars.

Another common kind of difficulty over identifying what it is ethically defensible to do involves the justifying of means in terms of ends. Obviously, the rationality of your choice of means relates to its appropriateness in relation to your ends. Acting ethically obliges you to vet both ends and means. Thus, even if an end is innocent, even praiseworthy, and even if the means proposed is appropriate, even necessary, for achieving the end, there may still be ethical objection to the means. Ethics sets constraints not only on what aims we may pursue but also on how we may pursue them. Thus, for example, even if your goal is disinterested, to protect loyal and deserving employees' jobs, that does not justify your falsifying accounts or bribing your accountant to do so, even if you can find no other way to avoid employees being made redundant.

On the other hand, actions that would normally not be ethically permissible means are sometimes justified precisely because they are in the circumstances 'necessary' – necessary in relation to some end. It is generally thought, for example, that you may be justified in killing another person if so doing is truly necessary to defend your life. There is then a problem over where necessity makes a means that is usually off-limits permissible. Might you, for example, be justified in lying in self-defence where it is not your personal survival that is at stake but the survival of your business – which, after all, is the source of many employees' livelihoods?

Compliance Problems

What gives rise to difficulties over compliance, that is, difficulties over doing what you know you ought to do? In some cases the difficulty is bound up with the apparent, if not real, divergence between duty and interests. Thus, it may be quite clearly your duty to be the bearer of bad news – for example, that targets proposed by the management are unrealistic or that a machine modified inappropriately (maybe against your advice) is not functioning efficiently. In the circumstances it may be obvious to you that your reporting this would be tantamount to career suicide: proverbially, the bearer of bad news often gets the blame.

When duty and interests diverge, it may not be self-interest narrowly conceived that stands in the way of duty; it may be – and often is – concern for others. It may, for example, be your duty to report on a colleague's alcohol problem if that is affecting his work – something which for friendship's and for loyalty's sake you are loathe to do.

In general, where doing as you ought requires heroic self-denial or sacrifice a fair degree of non-compliance is only to be expected. The responsibility for non-compliance by individual employees rarely rests just with them. The culture of the organization in which they work may invite rather than discourage non-compliance. If, for example, the rules to which you are supposed to adhere are openly, regularly flouted by your fellow employees and the company simply ignores this, it is not unreasonable of you to look on the rules as mere window dressing: you can expect to be considered a chump if you are scrupulous about complying with them.

On the other hand, no amount of managerial vigour in promulgating and policing rules can ensure compliance. There has to be a willingness and respect for the rules on the part of those who are expected to comply. Thus, if the disparities in pay within a firm seem arbitrary or unfair to those who receive less, they may not scruple to 'compensate' themselves by petty pilfering or other perk-creating deviance from the rules. What illicit extra they pocket in this way they may regard as no more than their company owes them. If the rules themselves or the company policies or practices that the rules support (for example, over promotion, hiring or firing) seem to be discriminatory or arbitrary, compliance will at best be grudging – the interviewee who lies about her age because she considers it irrelevant, and unfair of you to ask.

Sometimes what appears to be a compliance problem turns out to be an identification problem – because what compliance requires of you in a particular case may be uncertain. Rules do not apply straightforwardly in every circumstance. Where the circumstances are atypical, judgement is needed over how a rule applies. It can also be unclear whether a rule is meant to apply strictly or only as a general guideline: 'Always treat the customer with respect' – does this apply even to the customer who is harassing your colleague?

We have noted that problems over identification do not occur just where those who confront them are personally morally deficient; that, on the contrary, they are more likely to be noticed and pondered over by those who are conscientious and reflective. The same is true, at least in some cases, where there is non-compliance. Non-compliance is not always a matter of individuals' mischief or skulduggery. It may arise from misunderstanding, and decent people may be driven to it or lulled into it under neglectful management.

How to Begin

How should one begin an enquiry into the ethical and the unethical – how to tell one from another? Is not the difference a matter of common knowledge? Do we not all know the difference between right and wrong? And if we know it should we not be able to state it, to explain it? We have noted two kinds of difficulty. In order to cope with the difficulty of identification we need to acquire judgement. In order to cope with the difficulty of compliance, we need to acquire commitment. Now, both judgement and commitment presuppose certain qualities of character, namely, moral virtues. We may know the difference between right and wrong in a general way, but still be baffled as to what course of action is ethically defensible in a particular situation – whether, for example, to give an employee who has been performing poorly since his late wife's sudden death, the sack. We may be in favour of doing right and avoiding wrong in a general way, yet be reluctant to do right if the cost of so doing is acute – to ourselves or to our friends. What we need in either case is certain virtues of character. What these are, how they are acquired and why they are worth acquiring will be central to our enquiry. But in order to understand properly what moral virtues are and their central role in making sense of ethics – what it is and how it matters – we need to begin by examining some basic notions, which, though familiar, are difficult to give an account of.

Further Reading

On identification problems
See Nuttall, *Moral Questions*, chapter 1; Cederblom and Dougherty, *Ethics at Work*, chapter 1.

On compliance problems
See Plato, *Republic*, St 357–67. (The standard means of reference to passages in Plato is according to the pages of the Stephanus edition of 1578. It is customary to record these in the margins of translations.) See further Rachels, 'Egoism and moral scepticism' and Singer, 'Why act morally?', and relatedly on conflicts of interest, see Macklin, 'Conflicts of interest'.

On how to begin
See Midgley, 'The origin of ethics' and Solomon, 'Business ethics'; see also Warnock, *The Object of Morality*, chapters 1 and 2.

Study Questions

1   In what sort of circumstances, if any, would you think 'necessity' might justify your lying to a customer, to your employer or to an employee?
2   If the cost of doing your duty becomes severe, does it cease to be your duty? Can a course of action be both your duty and heroic?

2
Doing Right

Right and Wrong[1]

The distinction between right and wrong would seem to be an obvious starting point for our project of mapping the terrain of morality. These terms seem at once comprehensive and of central importance: everything that we do may be said to be either right or wrong, and, whatever else our map of morality tells us, it is going to be pretty useless unless at least it helps us to tell right from wrong.

Understanding the etymology of a word does not always help us to understand current usage, but in this case I think it is instructive to trace the origins of right and wrong. The word 'right' is related to the German *recht*, meaning 'lawful', and to the Latin *rectus*, meaning 'straight', and to *regula*, meaning 'a straight stick, ruler or pattern which acts as a guide'. 'Wrong' is a cognate of 'wring', which suggests a departure from a rule, what gets twisted, goes bent or awry. (Compare 'tort', the legal term for a civil wrong, which is connected with 'contorted'.)

This etymological connection with law and rule is significant. Even those who do not believe in a divine law-giver often think of morality as a matter of rules or laws. Stealing, for example, is thought not only to be against the laws of the land but to be against the moral law too. Lying cannot sensibly be forbidden by law (except when it is a matter of perjury) but it is held to be against the moral law nonetheless.

Defining Right in Terms of Wrong

An important point emerges from this. If we understand by 'wrong' what is unlawful, then 'right' must be understood as a merely residual category, what is left over, what is *not* wrong, *not* unlawful. The importance of proceeding thus can hardly be over stressed. The distinction between right and wrong can be profoundly misleading if we do not heed it.

Consider, for instance, the question of whether everything that you do is either right or wrong. The question is difficult to answer because it is difficult to understand; difficult because the meaning of 'right' as it occurs here is quite obscure. Are we to understand it here as meaning obligatory or as meaning permissible? If right is taken to mean required by a rule, and wrong to mean prohibited by a rule, then there is no reason to suppose that everything that we do is either right or wrong. Many actions may be neither required nor forbidden, such as playing golf, listening to the news, folding one's arms. In respect of such actions, we might say, the question of their rightness or wrongness simply does not arise.

On the other hand, if we take right to mean not forbidden by any rule, then it becomes simply a residual or remainder category for whatever actions are not wrong, not prohibited by some rule or other. On this understanding of right, right actions include both what is morally permissible (all right) and what is morally required (obligatory). Right understood in this way does have the implication that everything we do is either right or wrong, is either allowed or not allowed, by the rules.

Since talking in terms of right and wrong (and, for the same reason, of just and unjust or of ethical and unethical) generates confusion, we should avoid this vocabulary: it is troublesome and it is unnecessary. Instead, we could draw a three-fold distinction between actions that are obligatory, actions that are permitted and actions that are forbidden. Of course, what is obligatory is also permitted but the converse does not hold: I *may* fold my arms but I do not *have* to. If, though, we do stick with a two-fold classification it should be drawn between the all right and the wrong.

This point is not just a theoretical nicety. In conversation and debate people are often insensitive to this particular distinction between right meaning obligatory and right meaning permissible. People who say, 'It is right (or ethical) to pay your debts' really mean that it is obligatory to do so, not merely that no one can reasonably complain at the sight of your handing over what you owe. Thus, before we settle down to discuss, say, whether it is 'right' to whistleblow, we need to get clear whether what we are trying to establish is if we *must* whistleblow or if we *may* whistleblow. This use of 'right' is better avoided (and it is easy to avoid it). Meanwhile, we need to be alert to the ambiguity in people's use of 'right'. Thus, for instance, before we weigh into the debate over whether it is right to conform to indigenous business practices and standards when we are doing business abroad if these same practices and standards are morally unacceptable back home, we should first clarify what question we are trying to answer: are we asking whether conforming is all right (permissible) or whether it is obligatory (required)?

Making Sense of 'The Right Thing'

Now that we have taken note of the distinction between right meaning obligatory and right meaning permissible, we can see that the difficulty over responding to the question, 'What is the right thing to do?' may sometimes be that the question is out of place. Indeed, we can see that the definite article – *the* right thing to do – will nearly always be out of place, for there is nearly always a list of actions that are permissible, or right in the sense of all right. Yet, the expectation that there is in general such a thing as *the* right thing to do may be generated by the question that is often said to define ethics: 'What ought we, individually or collectively, to do?'. Of course, given a *particular* context the question may make perfect sense, as when you find yourself in a situation where it seems that you are obliged (or committed) in opposite directions, for example, to keep a confidence, and to break it. In daily conversation, you can sensibly ask, 'What is the right thing for me to do here?' where the context makes it clear that you are choosing among a strictly limited range of options (for example, whether or not to keep a contract seeing that . . .).

It is another matter, though, to suppose that a life of virtue must be one in which such a question is constantly before your mind: in which you ought to be continually addressing the question, 'What is the right thing for me to be doing here and now?'. If we substitute for talk of right action talk of obligatory and of permitted actions, it is easier to recognize that there may not be anything that is obligatory for you to be doing at every moment. The virtuous life need not be seen as a life in which every moment has to be justified in relation to some overridingly urgent quest, though that is, of course, how some moralists see it – those, for example, who hold that we are obliged to maximize happiness or welfare.

Mapping the Rules

There are broadly two things we need to understand if we are to produce a map that helps us to tell right from wrong: we need to know (at any rate, agree) what is wrong – what is a departure from the rules of morality – and we need to work out how to signify wrongness on the map. Let us ignore for the moment the former of these needs: it aside, the latter poses no small difficulty.

This might not be obvious. We might begin with the expectation that we could accomplish our task quite simply by marking off on our map the no-go areas, the wrong ways of proceeding. We would not need separately to map right ways of proceeding, since right, as we have noted, is in this context merely a residual category – in other words, any way of proceeding that avoids the no-go areas will be right. But our task is more complex. Thus, while there may be some areas into which we would say that no one should go on any account, there may be others where it seems, rather, that we should say that there are some occasions on which we are permitted to go into those areas, or even obliged to do so. Moreover, there may be certain people who have special roles that permit or even oblige them quite regularly to frequent certain no-go areas. Should we say, for example, that lying is strictly out of bounds for anyone on any occasion? Or is it occasionally permissible to lie, for example to protect an innocent person from harm, or even obligatory – as if the innocent person is under our care? Might you be regularly obliged to lie to do your job – for example, as an undercover policeman investigating fraud?

The rules of morality are not all of a piece and if our map is to be useful we need to have some grasp of the different kinds of rules that play some part in the judgements we make about right and wrong. Because rules are of different kinds we should not expect there to be *a* right way to map them.

Types of Rules

How rules are supposed to influence our choices of action varies depending in part on the kind of rules they are. Consider, for example, the kinds of rules that govern our choices in playing a game, for example chess. Some rules are definitive of how the game is played. We will call rules of this kind 'regulatory'. Playing the game according to the rules means simply: in compliance with these regulatory rules. They are comprehensive and absolutely binding, for example that the bishop has to keep to squares of its own colour.

There are other, 'guideline', rules that apply to how one should play chess but which we do not include among 'the rules of the game'. These rules relate to strategies that, in view of the objective of the game, which is to win, are necessary – for example, always protect your king – or advisable – for example, that you should bring your knights and bishops into play early in the game, reserving other pieces such as rooks and queen for later. Of these two kinds of rules, the regulatory ones are more fundamental: they function as constraints on the objective or objectives to which the guideline rules are aids. If you could ignore the restriction of your bishop to its own colour, you might be able to move it to a position to protect your king. But that is simply not allowed. The regulatory rules govern how the game is to be played throughout.[2]

Similarly, in the case of the rules of morality, we may draw the same kinds of distinction. There are regulatory rules that define which choices are morally permissible – for example, forbidding the use of force or fraud in the pursuit of one's aims. These rules are comprehensive and strictly, if not absolutely, binding. There are also guideline rules of morality, telling us what to do – for example, to defend one another against injustice and cruelty, to alleviate suffering, and to do unto others as you would have them do unto you. In morality, as in games, the regulatory rules are fundamental. They function as constraints on the objectives served by the other type of rule. Thus, though you might be able to stop your colleagues' being bullied at work by killing their tormentor or to spare the employee whom you are not promoting embarrassment by telling a lie, such actions may involve impermissible means – impermissible even though the ends in view are innocent or even worthy in themselves.

It is natural both in games and in morality to speak of *obeying* the rules where what is in question are regulatory rules. We speak rather of *following* or *applying* the rules where the rules in question are guideline in type. Wrongdoing relates most obviously to disobeying the regulatory rules. When philosophers speak of the primacy of the right over the good, or of rights as 'trumping' other goods, what they have in mind is the way in which the regulatory rules constrain how other rules of morality apply. In the next chapter we will look further into the nature of these other rules and the objectives they might be supposed to serve. Meanwhile, let us consider further the character of the fundamental rules, the rules that are supposed to determine what choices of action are morally permissible.

The Role of Regulatory Moral Rules

Regulations restrict choice. If they are justified, there must be a compensating gain for the cost of compliance, otherwise compliance would be silly, irrational. What purpose is served by the regulatory rules of morality? Whatever the purpose, surely it has to be something of universally compelling importance since the rules are supposed to be binding on everyone? There has therefore to be some necessity about them: a necessity that explains why everyone 'ought' to obey them. The rules of chess, after all, only constrain chess-players – we do not have to play chess. The regulatory rules of morality are supposed to govern how we live our lives, how we deal with one another. They apply to us all whether we like it or not.

Now practical necessities, necessities for us to do things, are
most readily made intelligible in relation to our purposes: it is
necessary to follow this road, rather than another one, if you
want to get to London; it is necessary to place this tablet in a
solution if you want to dissolve it; it is necessary to ring the
surgery before 10 a.m. if you want a home visit. These necessities
are contingent on particular aims that you may or may not have,
whereas the rules of morality give expression to necessities that
are supposed to give us reason whatever particular purposes we
have and whoever 'we' are. It would seem, therefore, that they
must relate to purposes that any of us is bound to have – at least,
if we are being clear-headed and sensible, if we understand our
predicament.

What *is* 'our predicament'? Simply this: we all share a basic
need to live in society, to live cooperatively with one another,
since we are by nature social creatures and since the life of man
where the conditions for peaceable cooperation are absent is, as
Thomas Hobbes famously puts it, 'solitary, poor, nasty, brutish,
and short'.[3] Thus, if the regulatory rules of morality consist just
of those constraints that we all need to observe if we are to live
in peace, then we can understand their importance, their universal
authority and why we have an interest in people generally taking
them seriously. But, of course, it is even then only rational for us
individually to conform to these constraints if others are doing so
too.

Objections to the Hobbesian Account

Some people do not much like this Hobbesian grounding for the
regulatory rules of morality: is it not based on a rather sour view
of human nature – the idea that our mutual dependence constitutes a 'predicament'; that we cooperate with one another only
grudgingly out of self-interested necessity; that in the absence of
the convenient fiction of a social contract, we would all be at each
other's throats? Maybe Hobbes does not have a particularly rosy
view of human nature. Yet surely those who do, have no less reason to acknowledge the need for regulatory rules. Our motives
for cooperation need not be all, nor even primarily, self-serving. Be

our motives ever so amiable, we still need to act within the regulatory rules and to know that others are likewise committed to them. It is good news if the graduates of our business schools are dedicated to revitalizing the economy – not so good, if they are prepared to lie, steal or kill in service of that fine cause.

A more serious objection to the Hobbesian grounding of the regulatory rules of morality is this. It is all very well to observe that we need to live cooperatively and hence to accept the constraints that living cooperatively presupposes. A solitary life would be an appalling alternative. But why need we assume that our mutual dependence extends to *all* our fellow humans? We might be selective in whom we choose to cooperate with. To be sure, within the circle of our community, we need to accept the constraints. But the Hobbesian grounding for so doing suggests no reason why we need to keep within these constraints in how we treat those outside our circle, nor does it suggest a reason why we need to expand our circle to include everyone.

Suppose, for example, we choose to exclude a certain group of people who happen to be relatively weak against the combined might of the members of our community – for example, illegal immigrants. We do not need to enter into contract with them, do not need to deal *with* them and whatever it might suit us to do to them, for example refuse to give them any legal protections against exploitation, cannot be shown to be wrong by the Hobbesian account. But, surely, it would be none the less wrong to treat them so. Does this not show that the Hobbesian account of the regulatory rules is fundamentally flawed?

Yet I think that there is compelling reason from a Hobbesian standpoint why we need to expand the circle of whom we count in our community to include all fellow humans (future as well as present?). Only consider: whatever should be the criterion whereby we draw a line between those who are to be counted in and those who are not, it has to be such as to reassure all those who are at present being counted in that they will continue to be included. But if the basis for excluding some is our superior power, that those whom we exclude are superfluous, pose no threat to us, do we not all have reason to feel insecure for our own futures? After all, who of us does not hope to live to a good old age? But old age is notoriously a time of decreasing power and increasing dependency. We cannot therefore rationally acquiesce in the drawing of the line so as to exclude people simply on the grounds that we do not need their cooperation.[4]

The Conditions for Living in Peace

What constraints do people generally have to submit to for peaceable cooperation to be possible? Basically, it seems, there need to be constraints on the use of force and fraud. We cannot rationally engage in cooperative ventures to our mutual advantage unless we trust one another not to act violently and unless we can take one another at our word. What we say we will do, what we undertake to do, has to be sufficiently reliable for it to be rational for us to plan accordingly: truthfulness is as necessary for cooperation as the renunciation of violence. We need, therefore, constraints both against wilful deception and against violence. But precisely how these constraints on force and fraud should be formulated is not so easy to see – nor even whether there might not be alternative adequate though incompatible formulations that could serve equally well in different societies.

How strict a rule do we need, for example, against lying? The simple strict rule, 'never lie' would seem to be unacceptably rigid: we can readily imagine circumstances in which we would not only excuse, but advocate, lying. Suppose, for example, that the only way you can protect some innocent people from murderous assault is by killing their assailant, would you not be justified in doing so? Suppose, then, that you find you can divert the assailant with a lie, so as to protect the innocent people without having to kill their assailant, would that not be justifiable? In any case, is it not implausible that we need a rigid rule against lying *as such* seeing as some lies are trivial? We might feel differently about murder: no murder is a trivial matter, hence a rigid rule against murder makes more sense.

On the other hand, were we to regard the rule against lying as merely presumptive in force: as if to say that lying simply requires a justificatory reason indicating why the lie is necessary, so to speak, the constraint would be far too feeble to make it rational for us to trust one another: it is so easy to find reasons why lying is necessary – to get someone (often, not always, oneself) out of a tight corner. Exactly how strict a rule we need depends on what degree of flexibility it is safe to tolerate. Whether lying in certain circumstances undermines trust may depend on people's reasonable expectations, which might differ not only from one generation or culture to another but also within the same generation and culture from context to context. Customers when they enter well-known and long-established shops with imposing premises expect honest advice, as they do not when they are haggling with a street vendor.

The point is not that provided people expect to have their trust betrayed, it is all right to betray it. Rather, we should recognize that trust can only be betrayed in circumstances in which trusting is reasonable – that is, where one is entitled to trust. If the use of deception in a particular context is conventional – not just usual, but accepted, such as bluffing in bargaining – then one is not entitled to expect that those with whom one is bargaining will refrain from bluffing. Of course, the mere fact that a practice is common does not by itself prove that it is accepted or tolerated. Shoplifting is common in some communities. Shopkeepers have to budget for it. But that is not to say that it is generally approved of or thought to be acceptable. It may simply be that people who deplore it do not see how they can stop it except maybe by Draconian, unacceptable measures.

The Need for Map Revision

Since how strict the regulatory rules of morality need to be depends in part on the attitudes of people that happen to prevail, that may change over time, we should expect that the map of morality which we draw to help us to find our way, to make choices that are morally defensible, will need occasional revision. For the same reason we can expect to find that a map that may have served our predecessors well stands in need of some modifications if it is to serve us equally well.

Yet because of the common needs and aspirations shared by human beings in all places and all times – what Stuart Hampshire refers to as 'the constancies of human experience and feeling presupposed as the background to moral judgements and arguments'[5]

– because there must always be the need for a shared commitment to the constraints that underpin rational cooperation, we should expect any maps that have been in use for a long time to be of considerable value to us. We do not need, therefore, to begin our own map-making from scratch. It makes more sense to take the map we inherit from our predecessors as our starting point, in the expectation that we will need to make some modifications but that much that is on it we will need to preserve.

Map Reading and Not Doing Wrong

Some things are wrong for anyone to do; some things are wrong for some, not for others, depending on particular circumstances. The regulatory rules of morality that we have been considering are supposed to mark off areas on the map that are no-go for anyone. Certain practices (involving force and fraud) are to be avoided whoever we are – our map of morality should hold this basic information, which is of relevance to all of us.

But a map also holds information concerning what it is wrong for some to do, not for others, depending on such particular conditions as where one is starting from, where one is trying to get to and how one is travelling. You and I, using the same map, may not be starting from the same spot; we may be heading in different directions and we may be differently equipped and burdened for our respective journeys: you may be able to travel light and on your own; I may be somewhat burdened with baggage and may be travelling in company; you may be young and fit – able to take the high road; I may be old and frail – the high road would be wrong for me.

Similarly, what the map of morality tells us it would be wrong to do will include specific proscriptions that apply to some of us (on some occasions) and not to others. Today, it tells you, it would be wrong for you to stay at home, because it so happens that you have arranged to meet a client at your office. My diary today is clear; the map does not tell me that it would be wrong for me to stay at home. The map tells you, who are a senior civil servant, not to make public statements about your political allegiances; it does not proscribe my doing so, I being merely an academic.

Thus, to be able to read the map, you have to bring to it certain information regarding your particular situation. You have to find where you are in relation to the map, you have to know something of how you are equipped for travel and also of where you hope to get to, where you want to avoid. The bare recognition of the ringed off no-go areas on the map will not be much use to you unless you bring to it important knowledge about yourself and your circumstances.

Socrates chastises people he meets who seem confident they know what is right and wrong and what goals in life are worth pursuing, although they are sadly lacking in self-knowledge and seemingly oblivious to its relevance. Aristotle insists that one is not in a position to find one's way in moral matters until one has acquired considerable experience of life – that one needs to acquire what we might call 'worldly wisdom'. They are both right and therefore we need to attend not only to the question of what should go on to our map if it is to be serviceable but also to the question of what skills and understanding we need to equip ourselves with if we are to be able to make use of the map. It is a poor workman, as the cliché puts it, who blames his own tools: let us not suppose if a map fails us that the fault must lie in the map and not in ourselves.

But even in the drawing of the map we need to bear in mind the circumstances of those it is supposed to help and to what purpose it is supposed to be of help. We need therefore to give thought to the concerns of morality and to the variety of circumstances in which people wanting to give due regard to those concerns are placed: we need to understand where they are starting from, where they may be trying to get to and what their circumstances make it possible for them to do.

So far we have not remarked on the concerns of morality beyond the concern to avoid doing wrong, which we have understood to require at least a commitment not to act against whatever constraints it is necessary for us all to acknowledge if rational cooperation is to be possible. But morality has further concerns – even so far as it merely concerns avoiding wrongdoing since, as we have noted, actions may be wrong owing to a duty that relates to an individual's particular commitments. And are there not still other concerns of morality that have to do with doing well, not just avoiding doing wrong? This will be the subject of the next chapter.

Further Reading

On rules of morality
See Denyer, 'Chess and life'.

On Thomas Hobbes
See Hobbes, *Leviathan*, chapter 13; cf. excerpt in Singer, *Ethics*, pp. 29–35; see also Hampton, *Hobbes and the Social Contract Tradition*; Kymlicka, 'The social contract tradition', pp. 186–96; Gauthier, 'Why contractarianism?', pp. 367–73.

On the contextuality of the obligation not to lie
See Jackson, 'Honesty in marketing'; Fried, *Right and Wrong*. An excerpt of Fried's book, entitled 'The evil of lying', is reprinted in Sommers and Sommers, *Vice and Virtue in Everyday Life*.

Study Questions

1   Can you spot, in newspaper and other discussions on issues in business ethics, appeals to what is 'ethical' or 'right' that trade on the ambiguity between required and permitted? If so, consider in each case which sense you think is more appropriate. Why do you think it so?

2   We have been comparing the rules of chess with rules of morality. In what ways do you think playing well in chess is analogous to acting well in life? Is this a misleading analogy? What may be said for and against this comparison?

3   How successful is the Hobbesian account of moral obligation? Does it manage to explain the importance of fulfilling one's obligations?

4   Can commercial espionage or staff surveillance be justified on the grounds of 'necessity'?

3
Doing Well

Above the Bottom Line

Doing wrong, as we noted in the previous chapter, involves departing from a rule. Suppose that you have successfully avoided doing wrong – you've kept to the rules: does it follow that you have done well? Surely not – not, at least, if the rules that you have kept to are merely of the regulative type. You are new to the game of chess, let us say. You have mastered the regulatory rules and in the game that you have just played you obeyed all these. Still, you were easily beaten by your instructor. You do not yet play well. It makes perfect sense, though, for you to say to your instructor, 'What did I do wrong?'. You know that you have not broken any of the regulatory rules – your instructor would not have allowed that – but you appreciate that there are other rules you have yet to absorb – guideline rules. Thus, your instructor might reply, 'Well, you should have brought your bishops and knights into play sooner', or 'Aim to get control of the centre of the board' or 'You should have castled when you had the chance'.

In this chapter we will reflect on the guideline rules of morality, the observance of which distinguishes those who act well, morally speaking. How are we to identify what these rules are? What is their role and how should they be represented on our map?

We should, naturally, be on our guard in relying on the rules of chess to elucidate the rules of morality. How game-like is morality? Is it, anyway, altogether unlike the game of chess? The analogy may mislead us – or, it may help us up to a point. We may find reason to drop it. Meanwhile, we should use it with caution.

Already, we may notice significant differences. It is easy enough, after all, to list the regulatory rules of chess: they are uncontroversial and the same for all players. We have not managed to list the regulatory rules of morality. We have only gestured at their content: that they restrict our use of force and fraud. Precisely what that means for you or me, we have not been able to say – except to note that it might sometimes mean something different for you and for me, depending on who we are and how we are circumstanced.

Here is another difference that we should also bear in mind. Once you have learned the (regulatory) rules of chess, it is easy enough to conform your play to them: doing so is a test of your understanding, not a test of your character. But conforming to the regulatory rules of morality, even though doing so is not sufficient for you to be doing well, morally speaking, is not always easy. It is not easy to inform loyal employees that they are being made redundant. But doing so may be quite plainly your duty. It is not easy, if you discover that you have made a mistake that it will be expensive for your firm to rectify, to report your mistake. Yet doing so may be your duty. What you need in order to do your duty when that is difficult is not intellectual or business skills so much as virtues of character – sensitivity and compassion *vis-à-vis* the employees whom you have to inform of their redundancies; courage and honesty *vis-à-vis* your employer whom you have to inform of your mistake. Thus, in moving from 'doing right' to 'doing well' we should not think that we are moving from sketching an account of the easy part of being moral to sketching an account of the hard part.

Doing Well

To understand better what is meant by 'doing well' we need to reflect on the grammar of 'good' – how it differs from the grammar of 'right'. 'Right' if used to mean 'permitted by the rules' has no comparative: one permitted action is not more right than another permitted action. But one action may be good where another would have been better. Right and wrong, meaning permitted and not permitted, are exclusionary terms: what is not right is wrong and what is not wrong is right. But your action may be neither good nor bad. You may be neither acting well nor acting badly.

A point of similarity between right and wrong and good and bad: none of these terms is ethical as such. All sorts of things may be described as good or bad or indifferent outside any ethical context. Indeed, so many different kinds of things can be called good – holidays, scissors, actions, moments to ask the boss for a rise or a friend for a kiss – that we may wonder how things of such different kinds could possibly share a common property.

The Meaning of Good[1]

Not only can such a wide variety of different kinds of things be called good but the same object, activity or person can be good as described in one way, and bad or indifferent as described in another. As G.K. Chesterton observes, 'if a man were to shoot his grandmother at a range of 500 yards, I should call him a good shot, but not necessarily a good man'. The same person can be a good cook and a bad swimmer. We really need, then, to consider goodness (badness, indifference) with respect to a certain description. Nothing is *simply* good or bad, it is a good x or a bad y. Whereas Italian accountants are both Italian and accountants, good accountants are not both good and accountants: rather, they are good *as* accountants.[2]

Thus the criteria of goodness or badness are determined in each case by the kind of thing that is under consideration. And you are only in a position to judge whether 'this is a good x' where you have at least a rough idea of what xs are or do. Terms like 'large' or 'real' are similarly opaque as against, say, 'red' or 'Italian'. You may know nothing of what that red thing is that you spy in the distance – it could be a red coat, a red fox, a red car – but at least you can tell that it is something red. It does not make sense to say of an x where you don't yet know whether it is a coat, a fox or a car, 'At least I can tell that it is something good'.

Despite the variety of criteria of goodness, we may all the same discern a common thread of meaning: the criteria of good kitchen scissors and of good nail scissors may be quite different, even incompatible. Still, there is something that both types of scissors *do* and the criteria in each case specify just those properties by which they do that well. This is in fact how Aristotle explains goodness: it relates to a thing's characteristic activity or function.[3]

Goodness and Choice

A plausible analysis of the meaning of 'good' should make sense of the connection between goodness and choice.[4] In general, people choosing *x*s will tend to want good *x*s unless there is some reason to the contrary, for example that they are too expensive. Yet it is quite possible for someone, in choosing *x*s, regularly to prefer bad *x*s. Suppose that you are employed to spot and remove defective biscuits from a conveyer belt. From your special standpoint, it is the bad biscuits that are choiceworthy. Notice that there need be no *disapproval* in your routine judgement, 'This is a bad biscuit'. Quite the contrary, perhaps, since if production techniques improved so that there were no more defective biscuits, you would be out of work. The point is that the criteria by which you judge biscuits to be good or bad relate to a certain standpoint, the consumer standpoint – biscuits are for eating. But your on-the-job interest in biscuits is non-standard. Thus, a good biscuit *for your purposes* can be a defective biscuit.

Sometimes the criteria of goodness are vague and indeterminate just because *x*s have various uses or functions. Correspondingly, there may be alternative answers to what *x*s are standardly wanted for, depending on *whose* standpoint relating to which uses one adopts. Compare the criteria of goodness that parents would specify for a good schoolteacher and the criteria that pupils would specify – we might expect differences at least of priorities. Similarly, with 'a good worker': is a good worker loyal first to his mates or to the management? Does it not depend on whose standpoint one adopts?

Implications for Ethics

If we follow Aristotle, explaining what a good *x* is by looking to what *x*s are for, we will have no difficulty giving sense to uses of good wherever *x*s have a specific function or role – as with an artefact, such as a toaster, or a biological organ, such as a kidney. Can we extend without distortion of meaning this line of analysis to less obviously 'functional' terms – for example, a good friend, a good way of life, a good person or a good thing to do? Perhaps not. But if it should turn out that we cannot, by applying Aristotle's interpretation of the meaning of 'good', make satisfactory sense of such expressions as 'good ways of life' or 'good things to do', it does not follow that Aristotle's interpretation is therefore flawed. It may just be true that such expressions are vague, even vacuous, unless given a special context.

Imagine if a stranger were to accost you, asking, 'What would it be a good thing for me to do now?'. How could you advise, in the absence of any information as to what the stranger wants to, or needs to, or can, achieve? Compare being asked for 'a good stick'. 'Good for what?', you would need to know. In short, the merit of Aristotle's analysis of 'good' may be its limitations – it does not make sense of nonsense.

Perhaps, though, we can make sense of good as used in the making of moral judgements, for example, as to what are good or bad ways of life. One way of doing so would be by reference to the role we humans have been allotted – a form of thinking that relies on there being a religious framework to our existence, life being a task or trial that we must do or undergo, as directed, in preparation for what comes next. If we reject that framework, should we also forgo talk of good and bad ways of life? Such phrases become meaningless unless we can attach sense to the idea of some ways of life being more or less choiceworthy. And then we need to explain choiceworthy *for what* or *from what standpoint*? Does morality itself provide the standpoint from which ways of life, people, actions, even motives, may be judged good or bad?

Doing Well and Choice

We have already found reason why the general acceptance of constraints on the use of force and fraud is choiceworthy: without this acceptance we could not live in a community, and – being the kind of creatures we are – we need to live in a community.

In other words, avoiding wrongdoing must be choiceworthy if it is simply a matter of conforming to the constraints on which living in a community depends. These constraints, spelled out by the regulatory rules of morality, have the effect of limiting the means by which we pursue our aims – whatever these aims might be. To make sense of the notion of doing well, as against just not doing wrong, do we not have to suppose that we have other aims or interests in life beyond that of being able to live in peace: we need to live in peace in order to . . . ? And if we rely on the analogy between chess and life, we might expect there to be some counterpart in life to the goal of chess. The aim in chess is to checkmate your opponent before your opponent checkmates you. It is that objective in chess in the light of which are worked out the guideline rules that govern good play. So, we might think, the rules that govern acting well *morally* must relate to the aim or aims of morality. But does morality have aims – and if it does, why should we consider these to be choiceworthy?

Does Morality Have 'Aims'?

Now, obviously, there is more to living well than merely living in peace. The guideline rules of morality that counsel us on doing well do relate to other concerns or aims beyond the basic need to live in peace. Living in peace is only a precondition for living well. But we should not allow ourselves to be misled by our analogy with chess into expecting that the aims or concerns of morality must involve achieving certain targets or goals. Secular morality, I suggest, does not posit any ultimate target-like goals.

A goal is, by definition, achievable – the destination at which one aims, the end point of a race. If morality set us aims in this sense, we might achieve its goals and then be free to get on with other things in life. But this does not make sense: we do not think of the concerns of morality over and above avoiding wrongdoing as of no further relevance for us once we have achieved certain goals in life. The concerns of morality are supposed to be of pervasive and continuing relevance for the choices we make throughout our lives. Admittedly, we might refer to certain of our ongoing concerns as our aims in life, governing how we aim to live our lives overall. The misleading sense of aims is that which suggests an objective that can be achieved, which is like winning in chess, the final point for the sake of which one has been striving. Acting well in a moral sense, at least from a secular standpoint, is not like this: if we act well, following the moral guideline rules, it is not in order to fetch up finally at some particular end point. There is no secular analogue to the pearly gates. Thus, in drawing our map of morality we should not be thinking that all who use it appropriately will trace the same route and arrive at the same end point. Our map will not indicate an end point, nor even alternative end points. Rather, the map will indicate the no-go areas and danger areas and areas to keep within reach, for regular access.

If it is a mistake to seek an explanation of doing well (morally) in relation to some supposed aim or objective, some end point, how should we make sense of it? Although morality does not have distinctive goal-type aims, it does have a subject matter. Not all of our concerns or ideals have moral significance – not, for example, my own aspiration to become slimmer: if I were to succeed, I do not suppose I would have in any way improved my *character*, become a better person. Contrast the aspirations to become less selfish or more honest: success on these fronts would involve character improvement. The concerns and ideals that have moral significance bear on our ability to lead lives worth living. Moral concerns and ideals generally relate to living well and doing well – living worthwhile lives. Later, in chapter 5, we will consider how far we can, or need to, give an account of what makes lives worth living. Meanwhile, we may note that concerns and ideals in respect of how we live our lives only make sense in relation to individuals who are rational agents – who are able to envisage and compare alternative ways of living and doing and to make choices in respect of these.

Of course, a concern that is not as such of moral import may acquire moral import indirectly: maybe I need to get slimmer to stay well and I owe it to my young children to preserve my health. Still, the need to keep slim is incidental to the concerns of morality as the need to be honest is not.

While the further concerns and ideals of morality (beyond the concern to live in peace) range over interests and aspirations that are thought to affect worthwhile living – doing well, not just not doing wrong – they are not *merely* concerned with doing well as opposed to avoiding doing wrong. Just as the ethos of a game bears on how we interpret the regulatory rules of the game where what would be an appropriate application is problematic, so too the further concerns and ideals of morality bear on how we interpret the regulatory rules of morality. In a team game such as, for example, basketball, it is accepted that presiding officials will not see fit to penalize for every breach of rules that they notice – to do so might render the game unplayable, or at any rate, unwatchable. In order to understand what counts as good practice in the game, you need to understand not just what counts as winning but what is the ethos of the game. The ethos reflects the characteristic concerns of the players, who do not aim simply to win, nor even simply to win through fair play, but to win through satisfying play. Of course, some regulatory rules will be clear and strict, and umpires are not entitled to use their judgement over whether to enforce them on every occasion. Which rules should be so regarded is also something to be settled by reference to what the game is played for, why it is played.

The rule against accepting bribes is strict: employees are not supposed to exercise judgement over whether or when to accept a bribe. But some of the requirements in company codes of practice are issued on the assumption that those who apply them exercise judgement in interpreting them. Consider this requirement in a code for engineers: 'A member shall at all times take care to avoid waste of natural resources, damage to the environment, and damage or destruction of the products of human skill and industry.'[5] This requirement only makes sense if one understands it to proscribe 'unnecessary' damage or destruction. After all, even writing a memo uses up paper, which is a product of human skill. Whether a particular using-up is wasteful is a matter of judgement.

Similarly, many codes of practice require protection of the health and safety of employees. But, either explicitly or implicitly, such requirements include the qualification, 'within reason'. Thus, again, judgement must come into play in particular situations where it is not obvious if a risk is reasonable or not. It would be absurd to declare that no risks can be reasonable. It is not a violation of the requirement not to put employees' safety at risk that you require them to drive cars, go up ladders or use electricity.

The interesting questions concern what risks are defensible and on what grounds. Is it defensible to increase risks in order to keep costs down? There will be cases and cases. It may depend in part on *how* the matter is decided – whether those to be exposed to increased risk know and agree, and, if so, with what inducement or pressure. Might it be ethically defensible to ask employees to take greater risks in return for increased pay but not to ask them to do so in order to avoid management having to make some employees redundant? Could it be ethically defensible to ask employees in a third world country to undergo health and safety risks that it would be unreasonable and illegal to ask employees in your own country to undergo? We will come back to these questions in chapters 8 and 9. The point of immediate interest here is that judgement may be needed even for avoiding wrongdoing, for applying the regulatory rules. Where judgement is needed, it is assisted by the guideline rules, which relate to the further concerns of morality.

Conflicting Duties and Moral Dilemmas

People commonly describe as 'dilemmas' any situations that face one with a difficult choice. For our purposes it will be useful to define a dilemma more narrowly. Let us distinguish two types of hard choice: those that are dilemmas and those that are problems. By a problem, here let us understand a choice between alternatives where whichever you do would not be wrong, but where moral considerations might tell in support of one rather than the other. By a dilemma, let us understand a choice between alternatives where whichever you do *appears* to be wrong.

A situation gives rise to a dilemma if it compels one to choose between seemingly indefensible alternatives – where whatever you do seems to be wrong. If the alternatives seem to be morally indefensible, then the dilemma is a moral dilemma – suppose, for example, that you are at the wheel of a lorry careering downhill and the brakes have failed. Suppose that you can steer to avoid a school bus but only if you plough into some pedestrians. Is it not wrong deliberately to drive into a school bus, but likewise wrong deliberately to run down some pedestrians? Yet here it seems you cannot help doing one or the other – you are forced to choose.

In a game such as chess, there are no dilemmas – no situations in which the regulatory rules conflict in what they require of you – but there are plenty of problems. The guideline rules do not conflict with the regulatory rules. The latter are counsels, not commands, and they apply against the background framework of commands. Should we understand the regulatory rules of morality similarly always to have precedence over the guideline rules? Does the basic concern to keep peace override any further concerns? If so, there will be no dilemma if the choice is between complying with a regulatory rule and acting on a guideline rule: duties relating to the former will restrict how you may pursue duties relating to the latter. The duty not to lie, for example, is of the constraint type and as such it restricts the morally permissible ways available to you for furthering your company's interests even though that is also for you a duty.

Another case: suppose that you are a member of a promotion committee in your organization. Your friend hopes for and expects your backing for a particular promotion but it so happens that you believe another candidate to be somewhat better qualified. Is there any conflict of duty here between your duty to the organization and your duty to your friend? In the circumstances you could only help your friend by *pretending* to fellow members of the committee that you thought your friend to be as well qualified – were you to be candid about your reason for supporting your friend, the committee would discount your support. But to pretend *in these circumstances* would be dishonest. Duties of friendship are constrained by duties of justice, such as the duty not to lie. Hence, there is no conflict between duties here either.

But whereas chess does not give rise to dilemmas (only problems), the rules of morality are not so neatly sortable into the commands, which never conflict with each other, and the counsels, which are always constrained by the commands. The regulatory rules of morality can on occasion impose conflicting duties. You may have promised to act as best man at two friends' weddings and find in the event that both have fixed their weddings for the same day.[6] It is impossible to keep both promises. Now, it does not make sense to say that you are obliged to do what you cannot do. Here we may usefully distinguish between your prima facie duty – what is your duty unless another duty overrides it – and your actual duty. The dilemma is resolvable in that, although the prima facie duties conflict, only one can be your actual duty. We do not, after all, regard every promise as equally binding.

In so far as your duties correspond to other people's claims, you might expect to find yourself under conflicting claims routinely. But competing claims do not automatically give rise to moral dilemmas. Typically, duties allow you a degree of discrimination over how and when you act on them. Even strict constraint type duties may allow you some leeway. The obligation to pay a debt, for example, can be discharged in various ways.

The claims others have on you may involve open-ended ongoing obligations: obligations that are non-dischargeable. Consider the claim that those to whom you owe money have on you – a dischargeable duty. Each time you pay off a debt, you reduce the claims of this kind – and it makes sense to aim to free yourself entirely of such claims. Compare the claims your parents, children or friends have on you. Each time you act dutifully in respect of your children, you are not thereby *reducing* their claim on you. Suppose that the claims on you of your employer compete with those of your family: the former asks you to spend more time at work or abroad; the latter ask that you spend less time away from home. You may be bound by your employment contract to fulfil certain tasks that now necessitate your spending more time away from home. If so, your contract imposes a constraint on how you are able to fulfil your familial obligations. Even if not so bound by contract, you might judge that it is advisable to comply with your employer's request lest you be made redundant and thereby rendered even less able to meet familial claims.

Whereas the regulatory rules of chess rigidly constrain what moves are permissible – the commands govern the application of guideline counsels – the analogy in morality between the regulatory and the guideline rules is not exact. While it does seem right to regard the constraint-type regulatory rules of morality as governing the application of other rules – and thus to think of certain duties, for example, the duty not to lie or not to accept bribes, as stricter than the duty to increase profit for your business

– this is only true in general. In this respect, morality is more complex than a game like chess. The same moral rule does not apply with equal force in every circumstance. It is always wrong to move your bishop off its colour – equally wrong whether you do so to avoid a checkmate or to threaten your opponent's pawn. But telling a lie is not equally wrong regardless of the occasion and circumstances – compare lying about a candidate for whom you are supplying a reference simply to get rid of a troublesome employee and lying about certain details regarding a candidate that would prejudice the enquirers unfairly and that you consider they have no right to know about (perhaps you are asked if the candidate for a secretarial post is a lesbian).

So, should we exercise judgement over when to tell a lie or when not to? Are some lies necessary, hence permissible or even obligatory? We will return to this question when we have explored the role of virtues in applying moral rules. Meanwhile, let us proceed on the assumptions that the rules of morality can be divided into those that are regulatory and those that are guideline and that typically, if not always, the regulatory rules govern how we apply the guideline rules.

What, then, should we say in respect of the dilemma we sketched to begin with, where we envisaged a person forced to choose between driving into a school bus or running down pedestrians – either way, it seems, doing what is plainly wrong, deliberately killing people? But whereas there is a moral constraint on intentional killing (although, most people will qualify this, for example, where killing is necessary for self-defence), there is not the same strict constraint against knowingly causing another's death.[7] There is all the difference morally between mowing down someone where whatever you do someone will be mowed down, and mowing down someone *in order to* do something else.

Paramedics might deliberately but justifiably speed past someone in need of rescue in order to rescue others; but could they be justified if they were intentionally to run over someone collapsed on the road with the excuse that they were on their way to rescue several seriously injured accident victims? The paramedics have a duty to rescue and might hesitate over whom to rescue where a choice must be made. That would be a problem, not a dilemma. Even if there were moral considerations that told in favour of one rather than another solution, whomever they decided to rescue they would not be acting wrongly. But even if one is acting on the duty to rescue, some *means* of rescue will be morally impermissible – ruled out by the regulatory constraints of morality: you may not kill one person in order to save the lives of two. Suppose you are attempting to rescue a child from a house, to which its deranged parent has set fire. Would it be wrong to lie to the parent if that were necessary in order to gain admittance? Surely not. It is this kind of case that leads me to conclude that while the constraint-type regulatory rules typically limit how we may pursue our aims even when these are pursued in the course of duty, there are exceptions.

Moral Dilemmas and Problems in Business

In business life you may encounter moral dilemmas but you are bound to encounter moral problems. You will encounter a moral dilemma just where it seems that whatever you do is morally impermissible: as if, for example, you believe yourself bound to keep a confidence told to you by a colleague but also obliged to inform others who may be otherwise endangered. Moral problems, as defined here, crop up routinely in business as in life generally. You face a moral problem wherever there are morally more or less appropriate ways of doing things and where which ways those might be is unclear. Perhaps it is clear to you that a particular confidence must be broken. You may then face a problem over *how* to do that – whether, for instance, you should break the confidence openly or anonymously, whether you should give warning that you are going to do it, and so on.

Representing Obligations on the Moral Map

We have mapped the regulatory rules of morality that define what is permissible and what is not as certain no-go areas, fenced off as out of bounds for all map users, wherever they are coming from or going to. Can we now add to the map indications of directions in which all users are advised to travel? The further concerns of morality, though, include obligations that are ongoing, open-ended, non-dischargeable. They should not be represented on our map as locations that must be reached but may then be crossed off. Rather, they should be marked out as locations within reach of which we should always keep, for visiting and revisiting.

We have already noted that the analogy between the rules of a game such as chess and the rules of morality is not exact. There is still another difference between the rules of games and the rules of morality: what reason, if any, we have to follow them. This aspect of rules – what makes a rule rationally compelling – is the subject of the next chapter.

Further Reading

On the meaning of good
See Geach, 'Good and evil', and Hare's response, 'Geach: good and evil'; see also Williams, *Morality*, pp. 52–61.

On goodness and choice
See Foot, 'Goodness and choice'; Williams, *Morality*, pp. 62–8.

On morality with and without a religious framework
See Williams, *Morality*, pp. 77–95.

On judgement in interpreting and applying rules
See Jackson, 'Common codes' and ' Preserving trust'.

On dilemmas and conflicting obligations
See Gowans, *Moral Dilemmas*.

Study Questions

1 Examine a corporate code of practice. Can you distinguish which of the items in it are strict regulatory requirements and which are advisory guidelines?
2 Are there any circumstances in business dealing in which you consider lying or bribing might be (1) morally permissible or (2) morally necessary? How would you support your view against criticism?

4

Motives, Moral Reasons and Compliance

Unethical Business Practice

Why do some people in business knowingly act unethically? There are two obvious explanations: either they lack motivation – they do not care – or they lack will-power. In the latter case, they will have a conscience, but it will not be effective. In the former case, they will not have a conscience. Sometimes, of course, people act in a way that they know is *said* to be unethical, but *they* do not think that they are being unethical: some job applicants, for example, may not have a conscience over lying about their age. They may consider themselves *entitled* to lie to defend themselves against what they see as unjust age discrimination. Similarly, employees who feel that they are not getting the pay or promotion they deserve may think that they are justified in helping themselves if opportunities arise, for example, by exaggerating their expense claims somewhat.

But not everyone who is prepared to act unethically and does not have a conscience about doing so is minded to defend their action as not really, in the circumstances, unethical. Some people are open-minded about whether or not to avoid unethical practices, depending on the consequences – whether people will notice, whether those who notice are likely to mind and whether those who mind are likely to be in a position to cause trouble. In this chapter, we will reflect on the attitude of those who are open-minded in this way about unethical practices: those who do not see reason always to avoid acting unethically. Are they in some way mistaken? Is it possible to show that everyone who understands fully the importance of avoiding unethical action will be motivated to avoid it?

The Price of Compliance

So far we have been reflecting on the different ways in which moral considerations are thought to be relevant to the choices we make, the practices we adopt and the policies we follow. Morality, we have noted, rules out certain ways of acting as 'wrong': it imposes constraints on our choices – which we represent on our moral map as fenced off no-go areas.[1] Morality also involves a commitment to certain concerns, which we take into account in our choices. Representing, on our moral map, just how these concerns are supposed to be taken into account in our choices is more difficult since we have a wide discretion over how and when we take them into account – there being no 'right way'. Thus, I have suggested that we designate them as points on the map that we need to keep within easy reach of wherever we choose to travel.

Obviously, both the constraints of morality and its concerns impose limitations on where we can travel: they are *restrictive*. What reason do we have to accept these restrictions? Notice that so far we have addressed this question simply from a collective standpoint – what is in 'our' interests, what 'we' need to do. From a collective standpoint, we notice how we stand to lose if we are not prepared to accept certain moral constraints in how we treat each other, how we benefit by considering ourselves bound, as it were, by a social contract.

But just because we collectively have reason, it does not follow that we individually have reason. While we individually stand to benefit if we collectively accept the moral restrictions, might we not individually stand to benefit even more if people generally are minded to accept these constraints while we individually seize on such opportunities as may arise to free-ride on others' restraint? It is, after all, the general acceptance of the moral restrictions that matters for each of us individually: thus if people do not generally accept these limitations there is no use, no advantage, in our individually doing so – you or I cannot simply through our own acceptance sustain the social contract that is needed to underpin living in a community. If, on the other hand, people do generally accept these limitations, the social contract will be sustained whether or not you or I individually accept these limitations. Hence, our appreciation of the importance to us individually of these limitations being generally accepted gives each of us individually no reason at all to accept them. At best it gives us reason to pretend to do so since we want others to be encouraged to do so.

Hume's 'Sensible Knave'

This discrepancy between what it is in our interests that others do (genuinely accept the limitations) and what it is in our interests that we ourselves do (merely pretend that we accept the limitations) explains the plausibility of David Hume's sensible knave:

> A sensible knave, in particular incidents, may think that an act of iniquity or infidelity will make a considerable addition to his fortune, without causing any considerable breach in the social union and confederacy. That honesty is the best policy, may be a good general rule, but is liable to many exceptions; and he, it may perhaps be thought, conducts himself with most wisdom, who observes the general rule, and takes advantage of all the exceptions.[2]

Yet if Hume's malefactor is sensible to take advantage of all the exceptions, do we not all of us have reason to be sensible malefactors? If all of us were to adopt such an attitude, only being minded to act within the moral limitations where the general rule applied – that is, where doing so happened to be clearly best policy – how could the social contract be sustained? Can you trust people to act within the limitations if their motive for so doing is merely indirect and provisional – and they *know* it? Maybe you do trust, because you have to: how else can you live? But the trust must be precarious if dependent on indirect motivation.

Plato explores the possibility that the social contract is sustained only through fear or ignorance.[3] That fear is what keeps us in check is suggested by the story of the shepherd, Gyges. According to the story, this shepherd, having happened on a magic ring with the power to make its wearer invisible at will, has no scruple about using his power to do evil with impunity: he gets himself included among a party of messengers to the king; he seduces the queen, murders the king and becomes king himself – the moral being: wouldn't we all do the same if only we had the magic to make ourselves invisible at will? To be sure we do not have the magic, but if we would do the same if only we did, does that not demonstrate that it is only fear that makes us just – that makes us accept the moral limitations?

People may wisely accept these limitations if the cost to those who are caught out deviating is sufficiently grim – if, as Hobbes suggests, they could expect to be made social outcasts. Hobbes observes, the mere fact that some people who take foolish gambles get away with it does not in the least diminish the foolishness of their behaviour. Yet we may question whether society has the power, or even the will, to make the threat of social ostracism realistic. We think of many notorious villains who evade severe legal sanctions by plea bargaining and whose notoriety brings in train lucrative films and books that tell their story. We note that society, anyway, is not all that homogeneous so that there are often going to be sub-groups within society whose sympathies are on the side of the offender rather than on the side of the officials imposing the law – for example, those whose sympathies are with the ex-husbands being hounded for excessive payments towards the upkeep of their children, or with the small businesses that fail to observe the labyrinthine bureaucratic regulations issuing from the EU. In such cases offenders who are caught may be ostracized only by a portion of society, and that a portion whose esteem they do not crave. We reckon anyway that only a small fraction of those who offend are detected – thus, even if you are caught this does not prove you were foolish to take the risk, it might merely show that you have been unlucky. We note too that the cost of being caught for many habitual offenders is not such as to outweigh the benefits – given the alternatives available to them (they may have little to lose: be housed badly, obliged to skimp and save just in order to keep warm through the winter, never able to afford a holiday).

Plato also explores the possibility that what keeps many of us from offending is ignorance: we are 'conned' by others into assuming that honesty is always the best policy; we are subjected to moralizing fables and rhetoric from infancy on, and many of us fail to distinguish the real natural necessities that limit what it is possible for us to do from the merely conventional imposed necessities that limit what we can do only in so far as other people enforce them. The ill effects of imbibing a large amount of alcohol are natural – physically, we are defective in being unable to indulge without putting our health at risk. The risk is no less if we imbibe secretly behind closed curtains. The damage we do ourselves is just the same. Contrast the ill effects of acting unjustly – for example, cheating your employee or lying to your customer. Here, the ill effect (if it consists merely of loss of reputation and its attendant problems) does not attach naturally to what you are doing, it attaches only if you are found out and penalty is imposed. Moreover, social sanctions will only be imposed against practices that are *recognized* in your society to be unethical: if the average decent citizen in your society sees nothing wrong with child labour you can employ children openly without hurt to your reputation.

It is to allay such misgivings about what reason we have to commit ourselves to living within the limitations imposed by morality that Socrates undertakes in the *Republic* to give a full account of 'justice', of what we owe one another – 'in respect of non-interference and positive service',[4] which will show that what is morally required of us is also rationally compelling – and not just for those who care about their social standing or who are unreflectively submissive to moralizing propaganda. Socrates is invited to show that justice (like health) is something that we have reason to cherish for its own sake as well as for its consequences, such as the incidental benefits that attach to having a reputation for being just.

What Makes Unethical Practices Tempting?

Plato's *Republic* is more memorable for the forceful way in which it poses this challenge: to show that what is morally required is also rationally required, than for the answer Socrates unfolds in the course of his subsequent discussion. Basically, we are given to understand that it is only worldly appetites and enthusiasms that tempt people away from acting within the moral limitations. Unworldly people who appreciate what is really worth striving for if one's life is to be fulfilling do not feel the moral requirements as limitations. For them, duty is not burdensome.

This line of argument has at most only a surface plausibility. To be sure, in so far as happiness turns on getting a substantial slice of the cake, one is bound to be in competition with others: the more they take, the less is left for you – and the same goes for worldly desires generally. In these circumstances duty, bothering about fair shares, is burdensome. Contrast your situation if your happiness turns on understanding some aspect of physics or mathematics, or on appreciating a poem. Here, your happiness is in no way threatened if others share your enthusiasm. You are not here competitors. The chances are that you are eager to recruit others to *share* your enthusiasm. If you are uncorking a bottle, you do not want all the world knocking on your door. If you are giving a lecture, the bigger your audience, the more gratified you are. Similarly, if you go to the theatre and admire the performance, you are saddened if the audience is thin. If you are aware that the rest of the audience is enjoying the play just as you are, you will be heartened, not jealous.

Yet, it is obvious enough that it is not *only* worldly motives that tempt us to act unethically. Plato underestimates how even the noblest and unworldliest of motives can tempt us to do wrong. Many are the instances of wrong-doing motivated by love – even love of justice. Think of religious wars.

Moreover, Plato seems to suppose that all those who act unethically are driven by their worldly desires, that they are ruled by their appetites and lack self-control. Yet it is easy to find instances of villains who display considerable self-discipline throughout their lives. Stalin and Hitler surely had an abundance of self-discipline. How could Robert Maxwell or Ivan Boesky have amassed their fortunes if they had lacked powers of self-control? Barbara Walters, in an interview for the American ABC network's *20/20* programme with Ivan Boesky's estranged wife, Seema, asked if Ivan Boesky was a man who craved luxury. 'Seema Boesky thought not, pointing out that he worked around the clock, seven days a week, and never took a day off to enjoy his money.'[5]

Is there a quicker, more direct way of demonstrating the folly of acting unethically? What is unethical, after all, must be unreasonable – from an *ethical* standpoint. But why adopt *that* standpoint?

Reasons and Moral Reasons

If there is a moral reason for you to do something, does it not immediately follow that there is a reason for you to do it? In one sense, obviously, this is a truism: there is a reason (moral) for you to do what there is a moral reason for you to do – just as there is a reason (horticultural) for you to do what there is a horticultural reason for you to do, or a reason (strategic) for you to do what there is a strategic reason for you to do. However, consider how reasons relating to particular standpoints, interests or concerns *give* you or me reason to do something.

You are pottering about in your garden looking for some shade in which to place your chair. A neighbour pokes his head over the fence and offers you a bit of honest advice: you need to prune your roses and it should be done thus and so. Now let us suppose that the advice is, from a horticultural standpoint, impeccable: all of the gardening books would confirm the appropriateness of your neighbour's advice – that is, for anyone who shares the concerns of horticulture as your neighbour no doubt does but you may not. Have you any reason, then, to heed this advice? Maybe so. Maybe you need to keep on friendly terms with your neighbour and it is advisable that his advice is not snubbed. On the other hand, your willingness to be advised on this occasion may encourage many more tiresome intrusions of similar ilk: perhaps it is better firmly, though politely, to decline the advice. In either case, what seems to be at issue is simply what reason you have to do this or that in relation to the things *you* happen to care about. (Perhaps, we should add here, though, that what you have reason to do depends not on your actual acknowledged concerns but on what your concerns would be if you were relevantly informed and clear-headed.)

Do you have a reason for doing what there is strategic reason for you to do? Does that not depend entirely on whether the strategy bears on *your* concerns? Thus, it might be a good strategy if you want to beat down the price of the desk you are negotiating to buy to hum and haw a bit over the price and, at least, not to let on that you were actually expecting to have to pay more. But whether you have a reason to adopt such a strategy depends on whether it matters to you, for you, to whittle down the price.

There is an important sense, therefore, in which you do not automatically have a reason to do what you have a certain *type* of reason to do. We can understand that there are reasons of different types reflecting different interests – what there is horticultural or strategic or, say, culinary reason to do (use plain flour, not self-raising if you are making Yorkshire pudding). Yet even if you are engaged in a relevant activity it does not follow that you have any reason to conform to reasons of the relevant type (perhaps you want the pudding to flop: if the meal is a disaster, next time your guest will ask you out to dine rather than asking himself in). The same goes for moral reasons. What from a moral standpoint you have reason to do, you do not automatically have reason to do. When a beggar appealed to Talleyrand, saying: 'Sir, I must eat!', Talleyrand is said to have replied, 'I don't see the necessity'. We need to distinguish the moral ought, which gives expression to what is perceived to be morally necessary or advisable, from the rational ought – from what is perceived to be rationally necessary or advisable.

Thus, in order to provide a motive for people to avoid acting unethically, it is not enough simply to point out that unethical action is unreasonable *from an ethical standpoint*. To give people a motive, it seems that we need to connect avoiding unethical action with concerns they already have – or concerns they would have if relevantly informed and clear-headed. Hence, the common strategy of moralists is to argue that avoiding unethical action is a matter of enlightened self-interest. In the context of business ethics, it is claimed that good ethics is good business. Is this cosy picture, that you do not have to choose between the path of duty and that of enlightened self-interest, that there is just the one same path, to be believed?

'Good Ethics Is Good Business'

Even if this is true, might it not also be true that on occasion bad ethics is good business and maybe even better business? The case against 'bad ethics' (going in for unethical practices) depends on the claim that unethical practices if discovered are disastrous for a business: that, therefore, a business needs to avoid them as a matter of enlightened self-interest. But we should not jump to conclusions about the folly of taking certain kinds of risks just because some who have taken them have met disaster: maybe they were unlucky; maybe they were taking greater risks than you need take. The reasonableness of taking a risk depends on how great the risk is, the cost of reducing it, and the gravity of the consequences if you do not get away with it.

The Risk of Discovery

This will vary from case to case, depending on the nature of the skulduggery and of the business, or the individual in business, engaging in it. If your contract with the company you work for is short term, why worry about discovery in the long term? Who knows where you will find yourself working in a year or two? The skulduggery to which you now find yourself party may not come to light for many years. Robert Jackall describes the philosophy of 'milking' a plant: that is, following strategies of management that yield immediate savings but with adverse long-term consequences for a firm – for example, making savings by skimping on maintenance work, not replacing stores, deferring as long as possible paying bills to suppliers.[6] Such strategies may not harm the prospects of those who adopt them – if they are adept and 'move on' in time. Jackall quotes from an upper-middle level manager in a chemical company: 'The guy who comes into the mess is the one who gets blamed, not the guy who milked it.'[7] Jackall notes, 'The ideal situation, of course, is to end up in a position where one can fire one's successors for one's own mistakes'.[8]

Of course, it is quite another matter if your deviance is immediately obvious to those whose trust you are taking advantage of. Hume illustrates how in many social dealings it is rational to act fairly, cooperatively, fulfilling our side of the bargain, even though we have made no formal contract and are not being policed: 'Two men, who pull the oars of a boat, do it by agreement or convention, tho' they have never given promises to each other.'[9] Clearly, in this case, it is *immediately* obvious to one rower if the other does not pull his weight.

But are there not many situations in business where it is not going to be immediately obvious if one side is taking advantage of the other, and – if we are careful and not unlucky – it may never come to light at all that we have not acted fairly? Are there not also situations where if the unfairness does come to light those who have been tricked will not be in a position to do us any harm? In some cases, those who have been tricked will not care to reveal their *own* gullibility. When it came to light that the Fayeds might have lied to the Department of Trade and Industry (not in so doing breaking any law) some argued that, 'The wrath that has been targeted at them would be better targeted at the officials who were so incompetent as to be duped'.[10]

The Cost of Furtiveness

Moralists emphasize the stress suffered by those who act unethically and who have to cover their tracks. As Sheena Carmichael and John Drummond observe, most people want to feel good about their work.[11] But not everyone, though, as they admit: some are 'out to buck the system'. Those who are, may not *mind* about having to cover their tracks. Not everyone finds furtiveness *disagreeably* stressful. Iago does not fret over the risks he runs in duping Othello. He positively revels in taking advantage of Othello's naiveté: 'The Moor is of a free and open nature, That thinks men honest, that but seem to be so, And will as tenderly be led by the nose, as asses are.'[12]

The Cost of Discovery

Whether taking a particular kind of risk is foolish depends in part on how necessary it is to take it: what risks do you run, what do you face, if you do not take it? The cost of being unethical has to be set against the cost of not being unethical. In some cases, you might simply have to go out of business if you are not prepared to act unethically. You may come to realize that the particular kind of business you are in is inherently unethical. Suppose, for example, that somebody convinces you that animals have the same rights as people; then there is *no* ethical way of running an abattoir – which may be the business you are in. In the circumstances the only way for you to avoid bad ethics is to go out of business.

Of course, it might anyway be good business sense to close down – you might see no future in a business that violates animal rights. But that will only be so if not only you, but the public generally, have come to recognize animals' rights. In other words, the viability of your business depends not on its avoiding unethical practices but on its avoiding practices that the public perceive to be unethical – which is not the same thing at all. A practice may be obviously unethical although its wrongness is not obvious to everyone. The attempted genocide of European Jewry was obviously wrong; but not everyone involved thought it to be so. The British air-bombing of Dresden in 1945 (killing in one night at least 80 000 German civilians) was surely wrong; but not everyone involved thought it to be so.

Those who stress the risks to a business of acting unethically, cite corporate tragedies – BCCI, Drexxel, Bhopal, Guinness. The bigger the corporation, the more important it is to guard its reputation. But what about a small business? It too may need to be careful of its reputation: in order to attract and keep staff, to maintain staff morale, to obtain loyal customers and to avoid costly litigation. Still, it has *less* to lose if caught out. It may reasonably take chances that would be folly for a larger business.

It is often urged by moralists that a business that does not anticipate social trends – the popular moral causes – loses out: 'The reactive role is the loser's role'. That may be so. But notice that it is only an argument for attending to popular causes. It provides no incentive to champion unpopular causes. If it comes to light that you have been discriminating unfairly against immigrant workers, this might actually win you favour with your customers. If there is public sympathy for women needing work, employ women; if there is public concern for the disabled needing work, take them on. But when the popular mood changes, you need to change with it. There is, besides, an anachronistic tone about warnings of how unethical practices, if discovered, destroy your standing in 'the community'. The truth is that many of us, nowadays, do not live in a community, buoyed up with the respect of fellow members. Rather, we are, many of us, anonymous, as are our neighbours – except perhaps if there is a national crisis, a catastrophe which binds us – temporarily.[13]

As for those who do mind about their personal reputation, who want others to think well of them, they may still reckon it is sometimes in their own interests to act unethically. You may realize that if your corner-cutting unethical practices were to become public knowledge this would be very damaging to your company. It does not follow that it would be a crazy risk for *you* to take. Maybe your job is on the line in any case if you do not meet certain targets the company has set. Maybe you see no other way to meet those targets but by cutting corners: 'It is probably also fair to say that the managers of the Exxon Shipping Company and the Alyeska Pipeline Service Corporation were not uncaring, uncommitted people who calmly accepted the inevitability of an accident waiting to happen in Prince William Sound. They were unable to take precautions against that accident because they managed the pumping, loading, and shipping operations under an ongoing shortage of funds and a continual pressure for profits.'[14] Exxon had been 'downsizing'. Hosmer reports one manager as having said at that time, 'I feel my neck is in the noose. If I don't deliver, they'll get someone else in here that will.' He quotes an Alyeska manager who said he was told, 'If you can't ship our oil and meet our budget, we'll find somebody else who can.'[15]

In short, while a business and those who are in business have some reason, often strong reason, to protect their reputation – to avoid, therefore, practices that are generally perceived to be unethical – that does not show that every business or everyone in business is unwise to act unethically. Enlightened self-interest may narrow the motivation gap between avoiding unethical action and acting rationally, but it does not close it altogether. It is easy to find chinks: situations where the risk of discovery is outweighed by the necessity of meeting a corporate target; or where the practice that you see to be unethical is not so seen by the public at large; or where there is little risk of short-term discovery and little motive for you to adopt a long-term perspective.

Virtues and Motive

There are people in business, as elsewhere, though, who face no motivational gap between acting rationally and avoiding unethical practice. This is because they have certain virtues of character and, in consequence, their aims and the need to avoid acting unethically converge. Those who are honest in character, for example, do not consider achieving their aims by lying or cheating. Being honest involves caring about being honest, not just because that is seen to be important for maintaining trust – though it is – but for its own sake. Those who are honest of character are committed to honesty: they do not depend for motivation to be honest on the indirect, social reasons for being honest. We noted at the beginning of this chapter that those who act unethically either do not care or lack the will-power to comply with moral requirements. Virtues of character supply both the motivation and the will-power. But does anyone in business have reason to acquire these virtues? What are these so-called human virtues? To whom are they of value and why? These are the questions to which we now turn.

Further Reading

On moral reasons and motive
See Plato, *Republic*, pp. 44 ff. (The standard means of reference to passages in Plato's writing is taken from the 1578 edition of Plato by Stephanus, whose pagination appears in the margins of all translations. The passage here referred to is from St 357a.) See further, Singer, *How are We to Live?*

On good ethics being good business
See Carmichael and Drummond, *Good Business*. See further, Solomon, *Ethics and Excellence*, chapter 8.

Study Questions

1   Compare the thought: 'doing that is wrong' with 'doing that will look bad'. Can you think of practices in business that in your view are wrong but that would not 'look bad' if made public? Can you think of practices that would look bad but that in your view are not wrong?
2   Can you think of businesses that prosper despite a bad reputation? If so, do people in those businesses nonetheless have reason to avoid acting unethically?
3   Do some businesses have a bad reputation *undeservedly*? Do *they* have reason to avoid acting unethically?

5
Virtues for Life

Practice

Our purpose here is practical: to provide a map or guide to good practice – by which, let us understand, practice which keeps within the moral bounds (as fixed by moral constraints) and which is compatible with moral concerns. To be useful, though, a map must meet (perceived) needs. A Guide to Good Pubs, however reliable its contents, will not sell to teetotallers. Who needs a map of good (moral) practice? Has everyone reason to be interested in the moral features of the landscape they traverse? Are the concerns of morality of concern to everyone?

The concerns of morality are of concern to those who have moral virtues. By moral virtues, let us understand dispositions of character that equip us for living well and for doing well: for having a life worth living. Of course, external circumstances may spoil people's lives however well they have equipped themselves. But even if external events prevent our lives from going well, whatever virtues of character we do manage to acquire will still enable us to make the best of our lot. Given that we all have reason to want our lives to go well, we all have reason to acquire moral virtues. But how safely can we generalize about what makes a life go well?

The Constituents of a Life Worth Living

It might be thought that any attempt to define moral virtues, since it has to appeal to a particular conception of what makes life worth living, is bound to be subjective, merely reflecting the views of this or that individual or group as to what are human goods or ills. Will not our own views as to this all depend on who 'we' are? Scanning the dispositions singled out by Aristotle as moral virtues, do we not find some anomalies; some doubtful inclusions, some odd omissions? Can we even agree among ourselves what to include? Will this simply depend on how culturally homogeneous 'we' happen to be?

On the other hand, reading what Aristotle has to say about the virtues, we may be more struck by the overall appositeness than by the occasional quaintness. Aristotle's project – to establish what are moral virtues and vices in relation to those traits of character that can be voluntarily acquired and that affect, for better or worse, our prospects of living well, of being fortunate – assumes that there are certain constant factors that promote or spoil our chances in life. Our need of courage, for example, relates to fear, an emotion familiar to us all, and one that we have got to learn to handle and control with judgement. Similarly, we need to learn to handle and control with judgement anger. We do not have to agree wholly with Aristotle's conception of what makes life worth living to agree at least thus far, that anyone's prospects of living well are significantly affected by the extent to which such emotions are tamed and shaped by judgement.

All of us are subject to these emotions and they seem to be to some extent educable. At least, that is what we suppose when we blame others and ourselves for failing to handle either emotion appropriately. If Jack bumps into Jill, not looking where he is going, Jill will *blame* him for his carelessness because that is a fault of character. If it turns out that he does not look where he is going because he is blind, blame is out of place just because blindness is not a fault of character. Since we regularly blame people for failing to control their fear or anger, we must believe that control over these emotions is something that can be voluntarily acquired. Thus, for example, parents and teachers of small children react to temper tantrums with carrot and stick strategies which would be quite absurd if children had no more capacity voluntarily to acquire self-control than they have to acquire control of the weather.

The fact that parents and teachers react in this way to children's temper tantrums – and always have done – reflects not only the common assumption that children are educable in this respect, that temper can be tamed, but also the fact that everyone understands the need in relation to living well and doing well. Irascibility is a trait that is both avoidable and that spoils, threatens to spoil or, at any rate, impedes, living well and doing well. Our concept of worthwhile living, then, may be affected by cultural influences but is not wholly determined by them. A guide to good practice may need to be rewritten, updated and modified, in the light of cultural changes, but the core of morality, what are the cardinal virtues, may be expected to remain pretty constant – as constant as is human nature and the basic necessities of human lives.

What are these constancies in human nature and human lives? H.L.A. Hart[1] points up the following five truths about what G.J. Warnock calls 'the human predicament':[2] (1) human vulnerability to bodily attack, (2) approximate equality – 'no individual is so much more powerful than others, that he is able, without co-operation, to dominate or subdue them for more than a short period. Even the strongest man must sleep at times, and when asleep, loses temporarily his superiority',[3] (3) limited altruism – 'if men are not devils, neither are they angels',[4] (4) limited resources – food, clothes and shelter are scarce and we have to toil to secure them, and (5) limited understanding and strength of will – we recognize the advantages of mutual forbearance but we still need sanctions to discourage malefactors. These truths seem to hold for all peoples in all societies. It is such facts about human nature that Hume has in mind when he observes, 'Human nature cannot by any means subsist without the association of individuals: and that association never could have place were no regard paid to the laws of equity and justice'.[5]

Virtues and Human Virtues

The virtue of a thing is what makes it good of its kind or what makes it do its job well. The virtue of a remote control device is that it enables you to operate some piece of machinery at a distance – to switch off your TV without getting out of your chair.

The virtue of direct debits is that they save you the trouble of remembering to post a cheque off every month. By definition, virtues are beneficial – though not necessarily to their possessors: the virtue of battery fed hens is that they are marketable sooner than those that are free range. That is a benefit to the farmer and, perhaps, to the customer, but not so obviously to the hen.

Human virtues, according to Aristotle, may be non-moral or moral. Examples of non-moral virtues would include intellectual virtues like being able to read Latin or knowing some trigonometry, but also other kinds of skills, like knowing how to sew or surf. These are skills that you may have and choose not to use – or even to misuse. Moral virtues, if possessed are used: they 'actually engage the will', as Philippa Foot (referring to Aristotle) says.[6] If you are honest, you act honestly. You might be able to read Latin yet botch your reading, and redeem credit for your skill with the explanation that you botched the reading on purpose. But you cannot rebut the accusation of dishonesty with the explanation that you were deliberately dishonest. Moral virtues, virtues of character, we take to be voluntarily acquirable. Hence, it makes sense to hold people to account for their lack of moral virtues.

Moral Virtues

Aristotle maintains that there are certain traits of character that we need to, and can, equip ourselves with in order to live well, to make the most of what life has to offer. We are not born with a fixed character. It is, we suppose, partly up to ourselves what character traits we acquire: those that help us to make the most of our lives we call virtues; those that hinder us from making the most of our lives we call vices. Moral virtues, so defined, are beneficial (vices, harmful) to their possessors – we have reason to acquire and keep them. Without them we cannot prosper; with them we prosper so far as external circumstances permit. Whatever talents or opportunities we have, whether we manage to put them to advantage or not, depends on our character.

But just *how* are the virtues supposed to equip us for living well? They play a crucial role in the choices we make, both by influencing what alternatives we consider, what we regard as desirable and permissible, and by enabling our judgement to be efficacious, in determining what we actually end up doing. The virtues enable us to see aright and to choose aright.

How Moral Virtues Involve Emotion and Judgement

In acquiring a moral virtue one is acquiring a disposition to blend emotion and judgement in a way that is mutually supportive so that emotions do not cloud judgement and judgement does not distort emotions. To have a moral virtue is to have a kind of emotional perceptiveness, rational desires – so that, for example, one is afraid only of what one needs to fear, to an appropriate degree, in a way that motivates an effective response towards the right objects and in an appropriate way; or so that one is angry just about those things about which one ought to be angry, to the appropriate degree, etc. Moral virtues are enabling – they enable us to feel as we should, to react emotionally to our circumstances in an appropriate way; they enable us to match our actions to our emotions. Acting well depends both on being able to feel appropriately and on being able to do accordingly.

Aristotle's account of moral virtues has often been mocked for treating virtues as means between extremes that are vices. This idea of virtues as means has a surface plausibility in regard to courage – fearing not too much and not too little as opposed, on the one hand, to cowardliness – fearing too much – and, on the other, to foolhardiness, fearing too little. There is not even a surface plausibility in thinking of some virtues – for example, justice – in this vein: hence Bertrand Russell's jibe – 'There was once a mayor who had adopted Aristotle's doctrine; at the end of his term of office he made a speech saying that he had endeavoured to steer the narrow line between partiality on the one hand and impartiality on the other.'[7] Russell is not here being quite fair to Aristotle, who himself points out that some names imply badness.[8] 'Partiality', as used here, would be a case in point.

Moreover, Aristotle also likens the virtuous choice to 'hitting a target'. This is a more fitting metaphor. It allows for the *variety* of ways in which one may miss – not just because one under-shoots or overshoots. Even in respect of courage, Aristotle quickly moves away from likening the difficulty of acting virtuously to that of finding a mean, to the richer metaphor of 'hitting a target', where the difficulty is not just one dimensional – whether one undershoots or overshoots – but where one may miss for a variety of reasons: one may be aiming at and hitting the wrong target, or hitting the right target but in a wrong way (e.g. cheating by positioning oneself impermissibly near to it). Thus, we should not think of modesty as merely not being overly modest or immodest (i.e. not modest enough): the virtue will involve being modest about the right things for the right reasons, neither underrating nor overrating one's achievements, but also seeing one's achievements for what they are and recognizing which, if any, one should take pride in.

The Centrality of (Moral) Virtues and Vices in Character

The centrality of the notion of virtue to our understanding of moral character – the kind of person one is – becomes obvious as soon as one starts to describe a person's character: virtues or quasi-virtues and vices or quasi-vices predominate – amiable; impulsive; senti-mental; prudish; good-humoured; surly; generous; mean; sneaky; devious; open; frank; churlish; rash; obstinate; arrogant; timid; self-effacing; brash; unreliable; loyal; trusty; frivolous; sombre – not all straightforwardly virtues or vices but at least suggestive of.

Not every avoidable defect of character is a vice: shyness, clum-siness and absent-mindedness are perhaps (usually) corrigible. They are defects which those who have them can take precautions over so that their having them does not get in the way of their acting well and doing well. Of course, any such defect may be a vice in respect of a particular role – clumsiness or absent-mindedness, vices in an airline pilot or a surgeon – and that just because in such a role the defect is bound to get seriously in the way of what the role requires. Moral vices, though, are pervasively damaging. The idea is that vices are bound to prevent one's acting well and doing well whoever one is, whether one is rich or poor; well or ill; young or old; whatever one's particular roles happen to include. We all need, for example, to learn to control our tempers so that we do not get angry about the wrong things or give vent to righteous indignation inappropriately – irascibility is a vice in anyone.

Quasi-Vices and Vices Proper

Acting well and doing well suggest a sliding scale: one may do quite well, rather well, very well. What we might call 'quasi-vices' can impede, but not very seriously. Consider, for example, untidiness. Someone who is characteristically untidy can be expected to act and do less well on that account – yet manage to do pretty well all the same. One may have compensating virtues for quasi-vices. Jack is untidy and Jill is tidy, but Jack accomplishes just as much as Jill because he is exceptionally industrious – he achieves as much as Jill does because he works harder. Garrulousness, is, maybe, another quasi-vice. In some roles and jobs, at least, it may not impede significantly. The hairdresser who gets behind because she talks so much, may conscientiously stay on after hours to complete the day's work. Her clients may not mind being kept waiting if they like her wit.

A vice proper as opposed to a quasi-vice cannot be wholly compensated for. A vice necessarily diminishes one's prospects of acting or doing well. People who do not have control over their tempers are a liability to themselves and their friends. Even their good qualities are tainted by such a defect. Jack may be loyal in intent, yet he cannot be counted on by his friends, for example to keep confidences, if he is wont to lose his temper. One way in which you might prevent a quasi-vice from spoiling your life and the lives of those around you is to rely on a friend or employee who is willing and able to make amends. You do not need to be tidy if there is someone to hand willing to tidy up after you. In the case of a vice proper, such an arrangement is not possible – you cannot rely on someone else to 'make up' for your dishonesty or bad-temperedness.[9]

What Character Traits Are Moral Virtues?

What count as virtues or vices depends on what count as goods and evils in life. As we have already noted, because of the constancies of human nature and human life, there is much that we can agree on here. Whoever we are, of whatever culture, illness, insanity, poverty, loneliness, boredom, insecurity and humiliation are evils. While, obviously, moral virtues do not protect us from these altogether, they do give us our best chance both of avoiding them in case that is in our power and of enduring them or escaping from them if that is in our power.

To be sure, there are also deep differences among us over what matters in life: the difference, for example, between the religious who believe in a Day of Judgement and a life hereafter and those who shrug off such notions as mere superstitions. But even between the religious and the irreligious, there may be much common ground over the dispositions that should be counted as moral virtues. As Peter Geach remarks, 'people of different religions or of no religion at all can agree to build and run a hospital, and agree broadly on what shall be done in the hospital.'[10] What we single out as cardinal virtues should be dispositions that can be seen to be essential for living well by both the religious and the irreligious, by both libertarians and communitarians.

Broadly speaking, there seem to be two dimensions to living well: the social and (what I will call) the aspirational. We are, by nature, social. We need to live in a community. Hence, we need to develop as virtues such traits of character as dispose us to be peaceable, and able to understand, cherish and uphold each other's rights. These social or citizenly virtues will include justice (itself a family of virtues, including honesty, loyalty and fairness) and what I will call 'humanity'. Humanity includes compassion but is a broader notion (humanity is, maybe, also best thought of as a family of virtues including, say, compassion, generosity and friendliness). Compassion is a response to others' perceived misfortunes whereas humanity is a response both to the negative and the positive experiences of others. Those who have humanity grieve over people's misfortunes and rejoice in their good fortunes.[11] By humanity let us understand something that is broader than friendship or even friendliness: concerning not just the way people treat their friends, the kind of interest they take in them, but something more general, the way people treat those with whom they deal – friends, acquaintances and strangers – and also the interest and attitude they evince towards the fortunes of those with whom they have no dealings, including characters in fiction and in history.

Communal life, though, is far from sufficient for living well and doing well. Bees and ants live in community, but their lives are unenviable models for human beings. At least two further elements are surely necessary for our living well and doing well: we need to live in a community that allows its members the prospect of expressing their individuality – space for each of us to make our *own* mark – and that helps us to achieve a sense of vocation, to find projects to pursue that give our activities a significance beyond the moment.[12] Both elements underpin self-respect: we need to see what we busy ourselves about as in some way important, worth the effort, and we need to see our own efforts as being distinctive – not just replaceable without loss by anyone else's.

The social virtues promote peace in the community. The aspirational virtues promote inner peace of mind, the sense that one has something(s) to live for, that one's life is going somewhere, is accomplishing something, that one has, or hopes to have, a quest, a vocation in life. No one would envy a life that offered safety and comfort but nothing more. Such a life could be enjoyed by an imbecile: it would not be fortunate or enviable. 'The need for purpose lies deep in our nature.'[13] Hence, we need to develop as virtues such traits of character as dispose us to find things to live for, to find ways of living that promise us a sense of personal fulfilment.

These social and aspirational needs are universal. They include features that are indisputably part of anyone's conception of what must be available for a human life to be worth living: the possibility of companionship, of security, of maintaining self-respect, of independence, of mental stimulation or challenge, of being able to give one's life a significance (being able to make one's mark, one way or another, for example on one's children, one's friends, one's colleagues). Anyone's life is marred by the inability to find companionship, by loneliness, by insecurity, by lack of self-respect, by dependence, by boredom, by a sense of insignificance.

Given that life worth living for any of us involves both the social and the aspirational dimensions – it has to be a life in a community and it has to be a life in which we have prospect of self-fulfilment – can we now state uncontroversially what qualities of character are obvious virtues and vices?

The Social Virtues

Is it not obvious that living well and doing well on the social front require an ability to elicit and maintain trust and also to identify others whom we can trust? The two standard virtues that seem most crucial here are dispositions to justice and humanity. Each perhaps covers a number of more particular virtues – excludes a number of specific vices. Each is vulnerable to other vices that indirectly threaten the virtue. Thus, Jack may sincerely deplore dishonesty and aim to be truthful in all his dealings, yet Jill may learn over time that he is not to be trusted because he makes promises that he means to keep but that those who get to know him find that he fails to keep and only believes that he will keep through self-deception. His intentions may always be honest but his amiability may be a kind of vice such that he is unwilling to face unpleasantness and so too easily agrees to requests without considering how people may be let down if he is unable to deliver. Amiability becomes a vice where it is not governed by judgement, where it is uncritical – as with those 'who think it their duty "to give no pain to the people they meet"'.[14]

Humanity, though, understood here perhaps as a sort of secular analogue of charity,[15] would seem to be a virtue that is no less necessary than justice for our living in a community. Justice, for example, includes respect for people's rights and fair-mindedness. But to understand what people owe their friends, what is fair between friends, one needs to have humanity. Humanity involves the emotion of sympathy. Those who have the virtue feel sympathy as they ought, when they ought, towards whom they ought etc. This enables them to understand not just how to treat their friends, but also how to treat mere acquaintances and strangers, how to respond or react to the fortunes or misfortunes of others, whoever they are – of animals, of fictitious characters, of future generations. Humanity, so construed, I suggest, is a cardinal virtue.

Besides the social virtues of justice and humanity, there are also the so-called executive virtues that make us more effective in achieving our aims, whether they are directed towards social or aspirational goals – temperance, courage, good-temperedness, ambition. In short, when we list the virtues we need for life as we know it, do we not end up pretty much repeating the lists that standardly have been produced? We need courage, as humans have always needed courage, because we encounter dangers and we prosper or suffer depending in part on the judgement and control we can muster in recognizing and facing the dangers we need to face. We need good-temperedness because as humans we are provoked to anger, and how we prosper or suffer depends in part on the judgement and control we can muster in recognizing what are grounds for anger and how it should be channelled and directed effectively and fairly. We need a sense of fairness because as humans we compete with each other not only for material goods but for the admiration and affection of others, and we need to acquire judgement and control in recognizing and respecting each other's rights.

Humanity has not traditionally been listed as a virtue, let alone a cardinal virtue. Aristotle is ambivalent. He says that friendship (*philia*) is a virtue or 'implies' a virtue and 'is besides most necessary with a view to living',[16] and he says, 'For without friends no one would choose to live, though he had all other goods.'[17] People have always attached profound importance to the capacity and opportunity for friendship: 'All I do know is that life cannot be understood without much charity, cannot be lived without much charity.'[18] Of course, 'friendship' does not describes a state of character. Friendship is one of the goods that the virtues put us in reach of. It is not itself a virtue.

But isn't 'friendliness' a state of character, and one that not only helps us to make friends, but also to get on with people generally? Do we not learn how to be friendly much as we learn other dispositions of character – by trying to be friendly, by imitation of those who are friendly, by studying, by observing, the difference between good and bad forms of friendship? Do we not praise and blame people for their success or failure as friends? Is not the difficulty of 'getting it right' in friendliness as with other dispositions of character not just a matter of being too friendly or not friendly enough but of generally exercising judgement in friendliness over how we support our friends, on what occasions, in what spirit and with what in view? Since friendliness is something we can learn and need to learn in order to live well; it is a moral virtue – or part of a virtue, humanity. Humanity includes friendliness but extends to one's responses to the fortunes of others generally, including those with whom one has no direct dealings.[19]

The Aspirational Virtues

It is, perhaps, not obvious which, if any, of the virtues that have traditionally been deemed cardinal have especially to do with the aspirational dimension to living well. The executive virtues, of course, are equally important to both dimensions. Indeed, if one were to single out one virtue only as fundamental, perhaps it should be prudence – that is, if we can shake off the association prudence has come to have with self-interest narrowly conceived. Aristotle singles out *phronesis*, often translated as 'practical wisdom' – wisdom in one's voluntary actions. He classifies this as an intellectual virtue, although he also regards it as an element in the exercise of any moral virtue. He carefully distinguishes *phronesis* from mere practical cleverness, competence in finding and realizing the means to one's ends, whatever these are. Such competence cannot rate as a virtue with Aristotle just because one would not necessarily be advantaged by it – not if one's ends were typically ill-judged. *Phronesis* involves both practical cleverness and wisdom about what ends are worth pursuing – not what ends are worth pursuing just in general, but what it is appropriate for you or me to be pursuing given our circumstances here and now and in the foreseeable future, and given our personal histories and natures.

Phronesis or practical wisdom, so defined, does not seem to describe any specific single disposition. Rather, it identifies an essential judgmental component in any disposition that qualifies as a moral virtue. Judgement is part and parcel of all virtues, whether social or aspirational. Aspirational virtues will include dispositions that equip us to find significance in our lives – things to aim at or work on that are worth our doing and in which we can rightly take a pride. Can we name some suitable candidates? I suggest that sensibility is one: a disposition to discern and admire what is fine and noble and to be repelled by what is cheap, shabby or shoddy. We might also include ambition (or, enthusiasm) – suitably defined to accommodate the thought that ambition is no virtue if it does not incorporate sound judgement about what things are a proper source of pride. Modesty (self-knowledge), too, might be included, understood again to incorporate judgement so that one is modest about the right things and in the right way. Those who have these dispositions will not necessarily pursue different aims or work than the rest of us; what sets them apart may be more how they set about their work, what they give to it and get out of it, and how they fit it in to the rest of their lives.

The vindication of the list of virtues here sketched is that they are equally appropriate to life as we know it or perceive it as to people with very different outlooks on life and different views on what constitutes worthwhile living. Contrast the outlook of Aristotle, according to which it seems that an enviable life has to be significantly public with an element of grandeur about it – a life in which you must make your mark and be remembered for it – with the Christian's promise that the meek shall inherit the earth, that God sees the little sparrow fall, that you may live well though humbly and apolitically. Contrast with both, a world view that is both secular and apolitical, according to which you may lead a quiet life that is all the same admirable and fortunate – memorable though remembered neither by God nor posterity. These are three fundamentally different outlooks yet all equally make sense of the character traits here mentioned as moral virtues.

The Interrelatedness of the Virtues

The categories of aspirational and social virtues are only loosely distinguishable. Aristotle and Plato held that all the virtues go together: if you have one, you have the lot. Whether or not we should agree with that, we can at least see how virtues in one category support those in the other. This is what one should expect given that a life worth living has both the aspirational and the social dimensions – that neither is sufficient by itself. Honesty, for example, is part of justice; it underpins trust – social existence depends on it. But honesty, in so far as it involves caring about, standing up for, what is true – caring, for example, that the beliefs one holds about oneself and one's fellows are true – supports the aspirational dimension of living well: one needs to have the disposition to recognize, face and hold fast to truths about oneself and others.

As we have noted, the so-called executive virtues seem equally important in regard to both dimensions, aspirational and social. Courage, for example, is needed both in carrying out one's social duties and in setting realistic but challenging goals for oneself and in persisting with these under adversity. Similarly, good-temperedness and temperance support both dimensions; they are enabling generally, making it easier for a person to overcome difficulties whether with themselves or with others. But these virtues are not merely enabling; they do not just make one better at achieving one's aims, whatever they are. People who can control their tempers can keep their cool whether their purposes are fair or foul. But if their aims are wrong, misguided, being better at achieving them is no advantage – which is why Aristotle writes in to his account of each individual virtue, *phronesis*, sound judgement.

Although the claim, made by both Plato and Aristotle, that all the virtues go together may seem to be contradicted by common experience – for example, of honest fools like Othello – as soon as one tries to isolate and describe particular virtues, their interdependency becomes apparent. There are certain common strands to the acquisition of any virtue: training of judgement, cultivation of refined feelings/attitudes (discernment/sensitivity), development of self-control (will-power). Courage may seem to be primarily a matter of acquiring self-control in the face of danger. But self-control *vis-à-vis* danger is only beneficial (hence helpful towards a life worth living) if one's feelings about what dangers are worth facing at what cost are sound and one's judgement about how and when a danger needs to be faced is also sound. Someone might be self-controlled and canny in facing a perceived danger yet be espousing an unworthy cause. One might face danger in a worthy cause yet face it ineffectively, ineptly, for lack of sound judgement.

The same holds for other virtues, for example honesty: you may fail to manifest the virtue of honesty through lack of courage (by, for example, not daring to oppose your manager who is telling you to lie to the auditor or to stand out against your colleagues who are plotting a cover-up). Likewise, modesty as a virtue requires self-control, suppressing the temptation to boast or exaggerate one's merits, and refinement of feeling, to recognize what qualities are meritorious *and* judgement, for example in appreciating to what extent one's performance on this or that occasion is dependent on good luck or the support of others.

Having a Virtue and Showing a Virtue

Virtues and vices are dispositional traits of character. To have a virtue is to be a particular kind of person, who can be expected to think and feel and act in certain ways. Thus, people may *show* a virtue or vice on a particular occasion who do not *have* the virtue or vice they show – it is not part of their character, their make up. Someone may, for example, be uncharacteristically honest (or spiteful) – acting out of character. But showing a virtue involves more than simply doing what those who have the virtue would do in the circumstances.

Suppose that you are not an honest person but on a particular occasion you do not lie: are you showing the virtue of honesty on *that* occasion? Not necessarily. Even if your boss tells you to lie and you refuse, it does not follow that you are showing the virtue of honesty – for that, your motive has to be appropriate. If you are merely telling the truth because you realize that the truth will out whatever you say, you are not manifesting honesty – nor, of course, are you being dishonest. Thus, to show a virtue on a particular occasion, you must not only act as those who have the virtue would, you must do so with appropriate motive or attitude: in the case of honesty, you must care about truthfulness 'for its own sake'. To have a virtue you must not only show it on a particular occasion, but show it typically when occasion demands or allows – it being a settled part of your character so to do.

Motives and Virtue[20]

Some motives are incompatible with any virtue, for example, spite, malice, jealousy and greed. The miser who risks his life to save his pot of gold does not display courage. His deed is reckless. Courage involves facing dangers that *need* to be faced. But there is no one motive that is 'the right spirit' in which to act courageously. Rather, there is a range of motives that are compatible. You may be spurred to a deed of courage variously, sometimes moved by compassion, sometimes by ambition.

Some virtues, though, do seem to require the presence of a specific concern. We do not jump to the conclusion that you are showing yourself to be honest just because you are doing as honesty requires – even if you regularly do so. Maybe you only conform out of apathy, timidity or lack of imagination. Being honest involves caring about being truthful – whether or not others will know or care.

Mixed Motives

Motives, of course, are often mixed. We help our friends out of gratitude *and* with pleasure. Should those who are virtuous always delight in acting dutifully? So we might suppose: if you really care as you should, will you not be eager to act dutifully? Yet there are circumstances in which acting dutifully with a heavy heart does not belie virtue – for example, informing employees that they are being made redundant.

Mixed motives for acting dutifully are not as such reprehensible. A society sensibly contrives to give its members more than one motive for acting dutifully: thus, if the sense of duty fails, prudence, solidarity or compassion may fill the gap. But when we are trying to judge someone's character, mixed motives complicate matters. One motive may mask the absence of another. We suppose that our friends are good to us out of friendship. But so long as our friendship is useful to them, we may have our doubts. Should we, for instance, credit whistleblowers with having acted from a sense of duty if they are known to have grudges against their employers? There is a catch-22 aspect to the whistleblowers' predicament. If they blow without first exhausting internal channels their deed seems irresponsible: they do harm without being able to show it was necessary. Yet if they do exhaust all internal channels before they blow, they must surely thereby have acquired grouses against their employers – if they did not have them already – since the employers have failed to heed their appeals. Thus whistle-blowers, it may seem, never deserve our respect: they either act irresponsibly or they act maliciously.

Egoism

The idea that there is at bottom one motive behind all one's actions, namely self-love, has had its advocates from the beginnings of philosophy. This view is called 'egoism': the idea that, as Hobbes put it, 'no man giveth but with intention of good to himself.'[21] This idea trades on an ambiguity concerning an agent's *interests*. Since you, as an agent, necessarily have an interest in whatever you do intentionally, it is easy, though false, to suppose that all your actions must be self-interested. To be sure you must in some way want to do whatever you do intentionally. You must see some good in what you do; see it as desirable – or else why do you do it?

Nothing follows from this, though, concerning what it is possible for you to want or care about. Nothing in logic precludes your genuinely caring about, and taking an interest in, for instance, the good of others. If in fact all friendships are fair-weather, all neighbourliness mere log-rolling, that is a fact of human nature which has to be established through open-minded observation. Once the claim that self-love is the motive behind all our actions is seen to stand or fall as empirical evidence determines, its persuasiveness dwindles away. At least, it would be more than a little remarkable should empirical evidence sustain the idea; when we consider for how long human infants remain totally dependent on others for nurturing, we must wonder how the species has managed to survive this long if, in fact, human affection is merely a sham.

Judging Motives

Our virtue is only put to the test where duty and interest point in different directions. You play a prominent part, let us suppose, in supporting a charity. Are you motivated, at least in part, by compassion, by sympathy for the plight of those whose needs the charity seeks to alleviate? So long as your charitable endeavours, of which you make no secret, enhance the image of your business, who knows?

Now suppose, all of a sudden, the charity you have been supporting becomes unfashionable – subject, perhaps, to prejudiced hostility. Your continued support for it may now stand to lose you custom. If you immediately withdraw your support does that only go to show that you were not after all motivated by compassion – you never cared? Not necessarily. You may have cared and still care but not so much as to put your business at risk: you may have other claims on you – from family, from employees, from shareholders – which rightly take priority.

Arriving at a fair and accurate assessment of someone's motives, including one's own, is fraught with difficulty. Often there are several plausible motives behind our actions: some flattering, some unflattering. The most plausible interpretation of an individual's behaviour is not necessarily the right one. People can act out of character. Because of the obscurity of motives and the importance of motive in the exercising of virtue, there is no easy and certain way of assessing moral character.

Importance of Character and of Motive

It is sometimes said that one's morality is something personal and private. Whatever one should make of this claim, it remains the case that we are (rightly) always interested in the virtues and vices of those with whom we have dealings since these are the key to what they can be expected to do or fail to do – for example, to the degree to which their word may be relied on. Jack may observe that Jill, with whom he trades, does nothing illegal, conforms to good practice. But can he infer that she is honest or at any rate shows herself to be honest on this occasion? To be sure, she does not show herself to be dishonest on this occasion. But maybe it never enters her head to consider what honesty requires and not because she is unquestioningly committed to honest dealing but simply because she is intent on securing Jack's trust and knows that he is in a position to check whether what she tells him is true.

Jack may wisely suspend judgement as to Jill's honesty or lack of it: her honesty has not been tested – not by her dealings with him, anyway. He does not know whether her practice is only accidentally good.

The same holds, of course, in respect of the actions of businesses. Why, for example, does one meat-producing business scrupulously conform to regulations prohibiting the use of hormones to assist growth while another does not? Is the former more virtuous, more honest? Not necessarily. It is true that the former is not acting dishonestly whereas the latter is. It does not follow that the former is being honest. A concern to be honest may not explain – not even in part – why the former conforms to the regulation. The former business may be simply 'going with the flow', recognizing that the consumers, rightly or wrongly, are hostile to the use of hormones so evasion of the regulations is too risky to be worth attempting. Does the former show more respect for the rights of the consumer, concern for the consumers' safety? Not necessarily. The business may have good reason to judge the regulation to be 'political' but unscientific. It may have clear evidence that the consumers' understanding is distorted, that there is no good health reason to ban the use of all types of hormones.

Check List for Moral Virtues

Let us now piece together the various features of the concept of a moral virtue. In this way we can provide ourselves with a check list against which to test what characteristics fall within and what without this account. If the account is to carry credibility we should expect it to make rough, not perfect, sense of our own convictions about what count as virtues, and of what traditionally have been deemed to be virtues. We should not expect it to make perfect sense since our own ideas about what are and what are not virtues – or what a particular virtue involves – are not clear cut. Is it clear that humanity, for example, is a moral virtue? I have made out that it is. But this may be doubted: is it, maybe, a virtue in some roles, but not in others – maybe not in business? Is it always clear to us what a particular virtue involves? We may be clear that fairness is a virtue but unclear whether fairness requires us to introduce affirmative action or whether it permits us to adopt a policy of last in, first out.

The account of moral virtues we have developed distinguishes them by the following features:

1   They are *dispositional* features of *character* (unlike, for example, being sickly, married or 43 years old).
2   They are *voluntarily* acquired – hence, lacking them is *blameworthy* (unlike, for example, having perfect pitch, or being good at holding one's liquor).
3   They involve acting with *judgement* – finding the mean (unlike, for example, being able to spell, or knowing who wrote *Hamlet*).
4   They are needed for *living well*, for making good use of one's opportunities (unlike, for example, the ability to play chess or to whistle).
5   They are *pervasively relevant* to how adequately you fulfil your various roles in life – as parent, offspring, neighbour, employer, employee (unlike, for example, being able to swim or to sing in tune).
6   They involve acting with a *proper motive* (unlike, for example, being curious, shy or energetic).

Applying the Check List to Humanity

For humanity to qualify as a moral virtue, all of the above features must accord with the account we give of it. Is humanity a dispositional feature of character? Is humanity a stable feature of some people's character, such that their reactions are predictably humane in various situations; for example, upon hearing of a colleague's illness, it is predictable that they will be finding ways to help, like offering to assist with the school-run?

Is humanity something we are born with or is it acquired by our own efforts? Do we not 'encourage' humanity in our children and chastise them for inhumanity – which would not make sense if we thought they had no more control over whether they were humane than they have over the colour of their eyes?

Does it make sense to think of humanity as calling for judgement? Do we not think critically about humane actions and try to guide our children to be discerning in their humanity – how they show it, towards whom and in what ways?

Is humanity necessary for doing well in life? Who would want a life in which humanity did not feature, whatever else that life contained?

Is humanity pervasively relevant? Is it needed for every role and condition of life? Here, perhaps, we may hesitate. On the one hand, human life is necessarily social – solitary life is possible, but it would hardly be living well. Even the unworldly Socrates, when he faces his impending death so equably, claims that death holds no fears for him as he looks forward to joining valued friends.[22] On the other hand, it may be argued that in certain roles humanity (or, anyway, friendliness) is inappropriate. If officers are friendly with their men, will this not undermine the necessary discipline without which an army ceases to function effectively? In a professional role, it may be necessary to maintain a certain distance in order to fulfil one's duty. Even the caring nurse may be warned against befriending patients. Yet if humanity is a virtue, it must be needed in every role. Thus, we would need to distinguish the friendliness the professional is advised against from proper friendliness – as part of humanity, the disposition that is a virtue in nurses, in army officers, even in prison officers. We would need to explain the difference between being friendly (humane) and befriending.

Finally, if humanity is a virtue, is there a proper motive from which those who show the virtue act? Those who show the virtue, we might say, are acting (in part at least) because they have a sympathy for those towards whom they are friendly. Those who find ways to help their ailing colleagues do so out of concern for their predicaments.

I have suggested that the awkward point if humanity is rightly thought of as a moral virtue concerns whether it really is pervasively relevant. Is there a way of explaining what this virtue involves that makes good the claim that this is a disposition that is necessary for us to develop whatever role we occupy – as needful for fulfilling adequately our duties as accountants or police officers, say, as for fulfilling our duties as neighbours or nurses?

Is there Conflict between Living Well and Being in Business?

There may, of course, be some roles, some careers, that are inherently in conflict with living well, with having virtues. There may, too, be some roles, some careers, that, while not incompatible with having virtues, expose one to special dangers. Some roles, for example, involve wielding much power, and power corrupts – not necessarily – but those who have it are at any rate vulnerable on that account. Interestingly, Aristotle, while he expects an enviable life to be one in which you distinguish yourself in public life, also cautions against worldliness and the pursuit of wealth or of political honours. Commercial life he especially disparages. There are of course echoes of this antipathy for commerce in Christian teachings. These sentiments notwithstanding, I will argue that there is no reason for us to regard being in business as a bad bet for living well and admirably – no inherent conflict between cultivating the virtues and pursuing a business career.

Further Reading

On the idea of a life worth living and human well-being
See Singer, *How Are We to Live?*; Hanfling, *The Quest for Meaning*, especially chapters I and II; Williams, *Morality*, pp. 87–95.

On moral virtues
See Aristotle, *Nicomachean Ethics*, especially books II to IV. See further, Foot, *Virtues and Vices*; Geach, *The Virtues*; MacIntyre, *After Virtue*; Slote, *Goods and Virtues*; Wallace, *Virtues and Vices*.

Study Questions

1   Is docility a moral virtue? If not, why not? Consider the following account of how Simone Weil claims to have been made docile through her work in a factory in Saint-Chaumond in 1935. She told a friend, 'I came out very different from what I was when

I went in – physically worn out, but *morally hardened*'[23] (my italics). Do you understand what she might mean by this expression? Do you think that a person could be morally stronger for being 'hardened'? What might it mean to be 'morally stronger'?

From a letter to her friend, Albertine (1935):

> Imagine me in front of a great furnace which vomits flames and scorching heat full in my face. The fire comes from five or six openings at the bottom of the furnace. I stand right in front of it to insert about thirty large metal bobbins, which are made by an Italian woman with a brave and open countenance who is just alongside me. These bobbins are for the trams and metros. I have to take great care that they do not fall into the open holes, because they would melt. Therefore I must stand close up to the furnace and not make clumsy movements, in spite of the scorching heat on my face and the fire on my arms (which still show the burns). I close the shutter and wait a few minutes; then I open it and draw the red-hot bobbins out with a hook. I must do it very quickly or else the last ones would begin to melt, and must take even greater care lest any of them fall into the open holes. And then I do it all over again . . . The first time, after an hour and a half of the heat and effort and pain I lost control of my movements and couldn't close the shutter. One of the copper workers (all very nice types) immediately noticed and jumped to do it for me. I would go back to that little corner of the work shop this moment if I could (or at least as soon as I have recovered my strength). On those evenings I felt the joy of eating bread that one has earned.
>
> But that experience stands out as unique in my factory life. What working in a factory meant for me personally was as follows. It meant that all the external reasons (which I had previously thought internal) upon which my sense of dignity, my self-respect, was based were radically destroyed within two or three weeks by the daily experience of brutal constraint. And don't imagine that this provoked in me any rebellious reaction. No, on the contrary; it produced the last thing I expected from myself – docility. The resigned docility

of a beast of burden. It seemed to me that I was born to wait for, and receive, and carry out orders – that I had never done and would never do anything else. I am not proud of that confession. It is the kind of suffering no worker talks about; it is too painful even to think of it.[24]

2   Which, if any, of the following would you classify as moral virtues? What are your reasons in each case?

- honesty
- compassion
- sense of humour
- patience
- modesty
- deference

3   Are some of the characteristics listed in question 2 more important for those who are junior in an organization, others more important if one is in a senior position?
4   Are some virtues and some vices more characteristic of men than of women? Are women more prone to dishonesty, and men to violence?

6

Reconciling Business Life with Moral Virtues[1]

Moral Hazards of Being in Business

Is there any special difficulty about having moral virtues and leading a life in business and commerce? Have we any more reason to suspect the virtues of enthusiastic and successful businessmen than of doctors, scientists or teachers? Maybe some occupations, though legitimate in themselves, pose a special threat to the moral character of those who engage in them.

One does not have to be a pacifist, for instance, to have qualms about the corrupting character of the military life of professional soldiers. They are trained to kill, to maim, to destroy property and to lay waste to whole regions of terrain, all of which requires that they learn to suppress the civilian inhibitions that are bound up with sustaining respect for life and for property. Moreover, as an army of individualists would be ineffective, soldiers are expected to do these things, if ordered, unreflectively, accepting on trust that the use of force is necessary, and hence legitimate – though the necessity on particular occasions may be neither obvious nor uncontroversial. Thus, even if a military career can be honourable, and may be outstandingly so, there is still reason to suppose that there are particular moral risks that attach to such a life: predictable situations that soldiers can expect to encounter (but which the rest of us are not likely to encounter) where certain virtues are severely tested.

Similarly, even if a career in business can be honourable, and may be outstandingly so, there may still be reason to suppose that there are particular moral risks that attach to such a life: predictable situations that business people can expect to encounter where certain virtues are severely tested. One does not have to be anti-business to have qualms about the corrupting character of business life for those who engage in it. There are, I suggest, two aspects of business activity that may engender such qualms: (1) the competitive nature of business: the seeming unremitting need to be doing others down, which might appear to be subversive of the concerns both of justice and of humanity (the latter also being a cardinal virtue according to the account I have given of it), and (2) the complicity of business in promoting consumerism and worldliness, which might appear to be subversive of the concerns of temperance (according to the account of this virtue that I am going to sketch here).

Competitiveness in Business

Disadvantaging the opposition, one's rivals, is not just an incidental feature of business life; it has to be one's purpose: to study the opposition, spy out their weaknesses, to take advantage of them, 'to steal a march', as they say – the military metaphor is perhaps indicative of the hostile attitude one adopts toward one's rivals: they are 'the enemy'. We expect enthusiastic and dedicated business people to take pride in, to delight in, their own successes. But inevitably their successes are others' failures.

Now both humanity and a sense of justice might appear to be impediments to avid and vigorous competitiveness. Humanity involves sympathy (compassion) where sympathy is due. The compassionate do not exult in the failure of others, nor are they indifferent to it – rather they seek to prevent or mitigate it. Those who have a sense of justice acknowledge the claims of the weak not to be taken advantage of and scorn to use their power to disadvantage them. Yet is not this precisely what the 'enterprising' in commerce are good at – spotting the weakness in the opposition and seeing how it can serve to strengthen their own position to the detriment of rivals?

Consumerism in Business

Temperance, traditionally, has to do with moderation of bodily appetites, a moderation which is supposed to reflect a low (and correct) estimation of the significance of the gratification of these appetites for living well. Its status as a moral virtue, Peter Geach suggests, is a 'hum-drum, common-sense matter'[2] – we need temperance 'in order not to be deflected from our long-term and large scale goals by seeking short-term satisfactions'.[3] Though, traditionally, temperance has been related primarily to moderation of bodily appetites, I will here widen its scope to include moderation more generally in respect of worldly pastimes and possessions. Worldliness, I will take to be an aspect of intemperance. It is a vice for the same reason: not because the kinds of gratifications sought are in themselves bad, but because they are beguiling and we tend to overrate their importance for living well at the expense of better things life has to offer. Now, it may be said that those who engage in business are especially susceptible to worldliness since their occupation is devoted simply to money making and since, moreover, the imperatives of the market require that whatever levels of profit they achieve, they never rest content but continually strive after further growth.

This suggestion, though, conveys a wholly misleading picture. Some people in business are self-employed, running a small business in which they may aim simply to make a living – to earn enough to keep going. Many people in business are making money for others – they do not own the businesses for which they work. And whether the recipients of dividends spend these on silly extravagances is no more business people's concern, it may be said, than is it the concern of doctors or nurses whether the patients whom they restore to health are going to lead worthy or unworthy lives. Admittedly, in making money for others they may get paid quite handsomely too – as, of course, do medical consultants and lawyers. If it is true that the rich are especially prone to worldliness, that is, then, an occupational hazard that is not peculiar to business life. In any case, arguably while riches may make one more susceptible to some vices, they may (as Cephalus argues in *The Republic* and

Aristotle echoes in the *Nicomachean Ethics*[4]) make one less susceptible to others – the rich are not likely to succumb to bribery, for
example.

Yet even if many business people live modestly themselves, are
they not, most of them, implicated in actively promoting worldliness, hence, as I shall argue, intemperance, in society? To be sure
not all business is so implicated, not even all trade and advertising. A business executive may be employed by a charity or be
working for a government service such as Citizens' Advice. The
advertiser may be promulgating health and safety; the salespeople,
marketing courses on environmental ethics. All the same, does not
much of business thrive off what John Kenneth Galbraith calls
'the dependence effect', creating a market for new products by
coaxing people into new desires, new dissatisfactions?[5]

Sellers, of course, do not have to believe in their own sales
patter. All the same, should we not expect that successful and
enthusiastic sellers enjoy their job and take a pride in it – which
is hardly credible if they believe, as it appears that those who are
temperate must, that anyone who falls for their patter is being
harmed thereby or is at least risking harm? It would appear, then,
that if there is a special difficulty over reconciling temperance
with a life in business and commerce, that is not so much because
those who engage in that life are personally liable to live intem-
perately, but because they are involved, generally speaking, in
exploiting and fostering consumerism, hence intemperances, in
others.

Towards a Reconciliation

To rebut the claim that certain moral virtues are impediments to
doing well in business, one might either deny that avidity in competition and in consumerism is characteristic of business activity or
one might undertake to demonstrate, by making a closer inspection
of each virtue, that avidity in competition and in consumerism, *in
so far as doing business involves either*, need not after all be subversive to any of them. It is the latter mode of rebuttal which I shall
attempt here.

Humanity

Humanity, I am defining as a disposition to respond sympathetically and sensibly to the joys and sorrows, fortunes and misfortunes, of others. It involves not just feeling appropriately, but caring, hence acting, appropriately. If you care about another's misfortune and are able to help, you are in some degree minded to do so. It covers, perhaps, a cluster of related dispositions rather than one, including, for example, civility, kindness, friendliness, mercifulness and generosity. It is opposed to a number of vices such as, for example, cruelty, meanness and spite.

Humanity is the term I am using to designate a sort of secular version of the theological virtue of charity. Now, if charity is construed as a theological virtue, it makes sense to speak of 'duties' of charity – duties owed not to the recipients of charity, but owed to God. Take away God, secularize charity into humanity – does it still make sense to speak of humanity as a duty?[6] If so, to whom is it owed? Of course, not all virtues need give rise to duties. Courage is a virtue. Doing your duty may require courage on occasion. But there are not duties of courage as there are duties of justice. All the same, those who have the virtue of humanity not only care about the joys and sorrows of others, they believe that one has a duty to care and thus, for example, that moral education of the young should include teaching them to care. Concern for others is not just 'a good thing'. To whom, then, is the duty of humanity owed?

Whereas the duties of justice are correlative to rights of specific individuals, the duty of humanity extends beyond one's actual friends, who do have correlative rights, to other people generally. Is it, then, owed to anyone worthy of sympathy whom one can help? It is not. Whereas rights as claims always imply duties (to do or to forbear), duties do not necessarily imply rights as claims on the part of others. Thus, though humanity is a duty not just vis-à-vis one's friends, those (apart from one's actual friends) who benefit from one's humanity are not receiving their due. Friendship, in contrast, is owed (literally) to specific individuals, namely our actual friends: they have a claim on us as a matter of justice. We do not in the same way owe anything to those who are not our friends although we might still use the term in a merely metaphorical sense to indicate the fittingness of responding to the joys and sorrows of others sympathetically – just as we might speak of 'owing' attention to a natural spectacle such as the Northern Lights, the haunting cry of the loon or a field of poppies in bloom: such things may be said to deserve our notice, our admiration. Those who have the virtue of humanity do feel sympathy – where that is appropriate – towards others generally in respect of their joys and sorrows. But it does not follow that they have a duty to help all those in need that they are able to help. They have a degree of discretion over whom, among those in need whom they could help, they do help. In other words: the concern is not selective, the way that concern is addressed is.

The duties of humanity and of friendship both involve imperfect obligation.[7] Imperfect duties bind us in an open-ended and somewhat indeterminate way: they allow us a certain discretion in how we act on them and they are not straightforwardly 'fulfillable'. In contrast, perfect duties bind in specific and wholly determinate ways and they are straightforwardly dischargeable – 'fulfillable'. Compare, for example, the imperfect duty of care parents have for their children with the perfect duty witnesses are under not to commit perjury in the witness box. The former duty is non-dischargeable – open-ended in the sense that, however conscientiously parents care for their children, there is always more that they could do by way of caring. The duty is also somewhat indeterminate in that there are many alternative ways of caring for one's children, and different ways that are mutually incompatible may be equally reasonable. Parents rightly and inevitably have a degree of discretion over how they care, provided that they care. In the case of perjury in the witness box there is no open-endedness, no indeterminacy (apart, of course, from the vagueness at the margin as to what counts as a lie), no scope for discretion: perjury is, quite simply, always contrary to duty. Witnesses can fulfil their duty whereas parents have never done 'fulfilling' theirs.

As, in the case of an imperfect duty, it does not really make sense to speak of 'fulfilling' our duty or 'doing' our duty, we should regard the mark of those who have the virtue rather to be that they are dutiful, that they act in accordance with the duty (from the appropriate motive, of course). There may be, as we have noted, various mutually incompatible ways of being dutiful and the fact that there are possibilities of being dutiful that we voluntarily pass up does not of itself show that we are undutiful. A doctor may be exemplary in his dutifulness in caring for his patients (caring in this case, of course, being a duty of justice, not mere humanity) though at this particular moment he is to be found idly strolling on a beach in Majorca while back home in Walsall, where his practice is, patients of his are dying.[8]

Now, since the duties of humanity are imperfect – allowing us discretion over how and when we show them – and since, moreover, they are not owed to specific individuals, might we not remove the alleged tension between being in business and being dutiful in regard to humanity as follows? Those who are aggressively competitive in their business pursuits exercise their discretion over whom they help and when, by excluding from their active concern anyone whose interests happen to be in conflict with their entrepreneurial interest. They confine their deeds of compassion to their private as opposed to their working hours. Charity and business, they may say, do not mix. But the same individuals who make a business prosper and prosper themselves thereby may be generous benefactors in their private lives and may devote their own time and energy to worthwhile causes (and, of course, be doing so because they genuinely care).

But this way of reconciling competitiveness in commerce with the duty to care will hardly do. Although the compassionate have some discretion over whom to help among those in need whom they could help, that is not to say that they can simply designate a whole portion of their daily life, their office hours, so to speak, 'off-limits' so far as compassion is concerned. Moral virtues do not admit of exclusionary zones. If honesty is a virtue, it must be needed and appropriate in all spheres of life and for all kinds of people, however circumstanced, be they young or old, rich or poor, workmates or playmates, superiors or subordinates, healthy or ailing, friends or strangers, and so on. Likewise with humanity.

Now you might, without noticing, not allow humanity to impinge on your business activities. You might be quite oblivious to the adverse effects your transactions or practices are having on others. The failure even to notice would itself suggest lack of virtue. The virtue of humanity sensitizes one to the fortunes and misfortunes of others. But suppose that you actually deliberate and choose to make it your policy not to mix humanity and business. Is adopting such a policy compatible with your having the virtue? If the policy is deliberated over, it must be chosen for a reason. What reason could a compassionate person have for adopting such a policy, namely not to mix business and humanity? If one knowingly chooses to tolerate the plight of the unfortunate, this must either itself be one's aim or a means to some further aim or a foreseen consequence of one's aim. The first possibility is surely ruled out for the compassionate: wanting someone's misfortune as such necessarily demonstrates a failure of compassion.

What, though, of the other possibilities? Cannot the compassionate choose to tolerate someone's misfortune, and even to cause it if it is the unavoidable consequence of or means to some other overriding aim? But, while situations may arise in which the compassionate who are engaged in commerce are faced with hard choices that they may resolve in favour of commercial advantage without necessarily compromising their virtue, such situations rarely do arise. In the normal course of business activity executives are not faced with such hard choices, since even if they are continually seeking to get the competitive edge over others, that is not to say that they aim at, or even expect, serious misfortune to result for these others thereby. Compassion, it should be noted, is only appropriate *vis-à-vis* serious misfortune: it is not elicited simply by disadvantage (not even if it is unmerited disadvantage). In all manner of ways we continually and quite innocently compete with one another for advantage; for example, when queuing for a ticket, we put all those who queue behind us at a disadvantage.

We compete not only in business but in sport, in play, in wooing. None of these forms of competition are off-limits for those who have the virtue of humanity. Having the virtue does not stop people from knowingly taking advantage of each other or from treating individuals in ways that are not 'nice', but it can make a difference to how they do it. It is not nice to make employees redundant – yet in order to remain competitive, that can be necessary. Imagine two managers, Jack and Jill, faced with the responsibility of implementing a decision to 'downsize': suppose that Jack has the virtue and Jill has not. Both will knowingly bring about significant misfortune for the employees selected. But Jack will have concerns and skills that will affect how he informs his employees. Being empathetic, disposed to respond sympathetically and sensibly to others' misfortunes, he will consider how to break the news and what help can sensibly be offered to soften the blow. He will show good judgement in how he handles the task. Jill, on the other hand, may not empathize. Even if she does, she may not be able to judge well how to handle the task so as to soften the blow. Her insensitivity may be confirmed by the way she chooses to inform those selected for redundancy – as if she decides to notify them by post rather than to speak to them herself – or if she foists the burden off on someone else.

The question of how people in business can square their avid competitiveness with being compassionate is misleading, then, in so far as it embodies the suggestion that the aims of the compassionate and of the aggressively competitive in business are characteristically in conflict. They are not. Those who are competitive in business do not normally expect, through their activities, to drive their opponents into ruin. Even where ruin is foreseeable, it will usually be a consequence not just of being outsmarted in competition but of other factors too, such as the parlous state of the economy and its ramifications – high interest rates, for example. Hence, even if a rival's misfortune is acute and was predictable, it does not follow that because one has contributed to it, one is responsible for it. Disadvantage may have been aimed at, ruin not.

All the same, while the aims of the compassionate and the competitive in business are not characteristically in conflict, they can on occasion conflict and force on business people hard choices – between, for example, abandoning a policy with consequent significant loss to those whose interests their business serves (shareholders, employees) and pursuing a policy that has a ruinous consequence for someone else. Compassionate business people may be expected to find such situations harrowing and to cast around for a compromise solution.[9]

Justice

It would appear, as I have suggested, that justice is an impediment to aggressive competitiveness in commerce in so much as those who have a sense of justice acknowledge certain claims of the weak not to be taken advantage of and scorn to use their power to disadvantage them, whereas the 'enterprising' in commerce are skilled in doing precisely that: exploiting the weaknesses of their rivals. Let us, then, consider more specifically what justice as a virtue involves; how, more precisely, it limits the exercise of power by the strong and whether on closer examination our suspicion is confirmed that those who are aggressively competitive in commerce must have especial difficulty in respecting the rights of the weak not to be taken advantage of.

Like J.S. Mill,[10] I would locate justice in that part of morality in which the language of rights and correlative duties is appropriate: it concerns what we owe one another and what we are entitled to require of one another. There is much else, of course, to morality that is not the concern of justice: attitudes and actions that are morally admirable or contemptible. Justice, as defined here, concerns the hard core of morality, so to speak; the constraints that are deemed to be an essential condition for living in peace and cooperation with one another. Basically, such constraints are in respect of force and fraud. Justice, then, is the disposition of character that attaches our wills to upholding and respecting these constraints. To be just is to recognize and embrace these constraints and to live our lives within them. Whereas if we lack this virtue we are either prepared to use force or fraud to gain advantage over others or, if we refrain, we do so only out of fear of reprisal or because of other inconveniences, if we have the virtue we characteristically[11] do not even entertain the possibility of gaining advantage in such ways and would dismiss the very idea with scorn if it arose.[12]

Those who are of just character act justly, as we have noted, for preference, not from fear or for convenience – but, because they are 'for justice', because they have a 'relish for justice', as Hobbes puts it. Because they are for justice, they will have a secondary concern: to see justice done – to defend and promote justice generally. Here, again, it is important to distinguish the perfect duty we are under ourselves to act justly – the primary concern of those who are just – and the imperfect duty we are under to defend and promote justice – the secondary concern of those who are just. In respect of the former duty, we have no discrimination over acting justly; we are bound always to act justly: not to lie, steal, cheat, murder when doing so is unjust, as it character-istically is. In respect of the latter duty, we do have discrimina-tion over if, when and how we promote or defend justice in the world at large.

Now, is it not going to be difficult for people who are keenly competitive in commerce, who are adept at exploiting the weak-nesses of their rivals, at the same time willingly to keep within the constraints embraced by those who are just? Is it not going to be difficult for the keenly competitive not only to demonstrate the commitment themselves always to act justly but also the second-ary concern to advance the cause of justice in the world at large? And is not everyone in business bound to be keenly competitive – 'driven by the Furies of private interest' which, says Marx, 'sum-mon into the field of battle the most violent, mean and malignant passions of the human breast'?[13] Marx claims that even though some business people have no personal relish for ruthless compet-itiveness, they are enmeshed in a system, whether they realize it or not, which involves their acting as if they are out to do every-one down.

Just how difficult it is to promote the duties of justice alongside avid competitiveness in commerce depends partly, of course, on what precisely these duties encompass. Here let us confine our attention to an uncontroversially central aspect of these duties, which would appear to constitute a substantial impediment to avid competitiveness – the requirement to be honest. Deceptive practices may appear to be so much a part and parcel of daily business life as to indicate that the combination of living virtu-ously and engaging in business life is not just difficult, it is down-right impossible.

This bleak suspicion perhaps rests at least in part on the casual assumption that deception in any shape or form is dishonest. But is this true? To be sure, there are many familiar kinds of situations in our commercial (as in our social) dealings where it is advant-ageous and also is common practice both to allow and even to cause other people's deception. We should not leap to the conclu-sion from this that all these deceptive practices are dishonest. Trust is the good that makes honesty a virtue.[14] But not all deceptions, not even all intentional deceptions, involve an abuse or betrayal of trust. Trust is abused only where people are entitled to rely on you and you let them down; betrayed, only in circumstances where (1) people are entitled to rely on you and (2) they actually do so – and you let them down.

Thus, there are all sorts of stratagems and tricks that we play on one another, not just in business but generally in our social lives, which are innocent although they involve allowing or causing deception: innocent, because trust is not being abused or betrayed. Is it dishonest to allow someone with whom you are chatting to believe that he is interesting you or amusing you? Does an honest person continually butt in to other people's conversations to correct misunderstandings?

If honesty requires of those who possess it that they eschew deception altogether, then the honest must be rather boring, tiresome companions and, moreover, incapable of close friendship: do we not need to harbour and indulge some conceits about one another to sustain affection and fellowship? Virtues, Hume argues, must be amiable qualities such as make us useful or agreeable.[15] Well, those who eschew deception altogether can be neither useful nor agreeable – certainly not the latter. Thus, if honesty does indeed require a complete renunciation of deception, it should go the way of the 'monkish' virtues, which, says Hume, are 'everywhere rejected by men of sense' and 'we justly, therefore, transfer them to the opposite column, and place them in the catalogue of vices.'[16] As in social life, so in business, we often innocently allow or cause deception. Accordingly, if we agree that it is not possible, and perhaps not even desirable, to do business without regular recourse to deception, we need not on that account concede that there is ever any necessity to act dishonestly.

Now, whether a particular type of deception that occurs in business is dishonest is not always obvious. We will consider some problematic cases later. Meanwhile, let us note that even though being honest does not preclude knowingly engaging in some deceptive practices, it does preclude engaging in deceptions that abuse trust. And does this not put those who are honest at a competitive disadvantage *vis-à-vis* those who are morally less fastidious? Other things being equal, the better armed in combat should fare better. The morally scrupulous forswear a weapon that their opponents are prepared to use. Moralizers may protest that the weapon in question is double-edged. But that might be reason to use it with caution and only as a last resort rather than a reason to rule it out altogether.

We should, then, admit that it can be more difficult to be effectively competitive if one is honest: yet maybe not significantly so. Obstacles that are self-imposed rather than externally imposed are more easily faced and surmounted. For those who are honest, the constraints that virtue imposes are willingly embraced. Those who are both honest and keenly competitive can be expected to exercise their resourcefulness in finding alternative ways of promoting growth that do not require the abuse of trust.[17]

Nor should we assume that those who are not honest automatically have the competitive edge over those who are. Although they are not bound by the same constraint and so are prepared to consider doing things that are simply out of the question for the honest, their greater freedom does not necessarily give them greater power. One obvious way of making ourselves stronger in competition is to form alliances with others. Those who are conspicuously honest should find it easier to form alliances – especially if it is reasonable to assume that having the virtue makes one better at recognizing its presence or absence in others. Here, again, we should note the importance in our account of moral virtues of judgement – that each virtue involves the exercise and influence of judgement. Honesty as a virtue is not to be identified with mere lack of guile, with the innocence of Shakespeare's honest, but utterly gullible, fools. To ally oneself in business with such persons would only make one more vulnerable to the opposition. Honesty as a virtue must be discerning and wise. The childlike simplicity of those who are unguarded and unsuspecting is not what one needs to live well and do well.

Obviously, those who are honest and keenly competitive in commerce will demonstrate their attachment to honesty not only by their own scrupulous avoidance of deceptive practice which abuse trust but also by their secondary concern: their readiness to oppose and expose the dishonest practices of others. We have noted that humanity is a duty but is not owed to specific individuals and, because it is an imperfect duty, we have some discretion too over how we help those whom we do help. Still, there is truth in the saying that 'Charity begins at home'. Those who have compassion will want to exercise it where they are in a position to do so effectively, which will normally include the home front. Hence, a conspicuous absence of charity there rather belies the presence of genuine concern. For similar reasons, we can expect those who are honest in business to be outspoken in their opposition to dishonest business practices perpetrated by others under their own noses, and effectively vigilant against such practices as they encounter. Honest people have a primary concern not to be party to blackmail and a secondary concern that nobody is subjected to blackmail. Thus, if someone initiates a commercial venture that leaves people wide-open to blackmail (like, for example, Barrie Goulding's use of closed circuit TV footage to compose the commercial film *Caught in the Act*), their honesty is rightly questioned. Someone who is honest will not be minded to think: it is a commercial venture; it is not illegal – so it is not unethical.

Temperance

What are we to understand by temperance? Is it appropriate to include it among Hume's 'monkish' virtues? And if it is, should we, like Hume, list it among the vices, not the virtues? Does being temperate require disdain, simply, for bodily pleasures or, more generally, for worldly pleasures and pursuits? Does being temperate require moderation or abstinence? Hume's denunciation of the monkish virtues, of habits of self-denial that go beyond mere self-discipline, points up the need to supply an account of the good that temperance as a virtue might serve: self-denial 'for its own sake' so to speak, would appear to lack merit or even sense. Let me quote more fully what Hume has to say against these 'virtues':

> Celibacy, fasting, penance, mortification, self-denial, humility, silence, solitude, and the whole train of monkish virtues; for what reason are they everywhere rejected by men of sense, but because they serve to no manner of purpose; neither advance a man's fortune in the world, nor render him a more valuable member of society; neither qualify him for entertainment of company, nor increase his power of self-enjoyment? We observe, on the contrary, that they cross all these desirable

ends; stupefy the understanding and harden the heart, obscure the fancy and sour the temper. We justly, therefore, transfer them to the opposite column, and place them in the catalogue of vices; nor has any superstition force enough among men of the world, to pervert entirely these natural sentiments. A gloomy, hair-brained enthusiast, after his death, may have a place in the calendar; but will scarcely ever be admitted, when alive, into intimacy and society, except by those who are as delirious and dismal as himself.[18]

Perhaps, though, we can recast our definition of temperance in a more Aristotelian mould so as both to salvage it as a virtue and render it a trait compatible with some degree, a modicum, of worldliness – of attachment to transitory pleasures, amusements and entertainments in life. The temperate person, according to Aristotle, desires (bodily) pleasures 'only to a moderate degree, and not more than he should, nor when he should not, and so on; but the things that, being pleasant, make for health and good condition, he will desire moderately and as he should, and also the pleasant things if they are not hindrances to these ends, or contrary to what is noble, or beyond his means'.[19]

On this account, temperance is not simply a matter of exercising self-control *vis-à-vis* bodily desires (or, I would add, worldly pursuits generally) but of possessing and showing sound judgement in the degree of importance we attach to these in our lives. A hedonist might display remarkable self-discipline, fasting for a feast; such behaviour would not manifest and might even belie the presence of virtue as pleasures would be foregone only for the sake of more pleasures of a similarly worldly type, and the effort involved in fasting might itself be a distraction from more important concerns. To this extent, I suggest, we should follow Plato who, in the *Phaedo*, repudiates the conception of temperance in which self-control is dictated merely by the appetite for maximum overall self-indulgence.[20] As with the virtues of humanity and justice, so with temperance, having the virtue is not simply a matter of acting appropriately. It is also a matter of acting with appropriate motivation – not, therefore, so as to achieve maximum overall indulgence – the hedonist's motivation for self-discipline – but because it is appreciated that these indulgences can easily absorb more of our attention then they merit and at the expense of other valuable kinds of experiences and pursuits without which our lives would be impoverished. My reason for extending the scope of temperance to include more than good sense in respect of bodily appetites is that it seems as important and for the same kind of reason to acquire self-control and judgement *vis-à-vis* other forms of pleasures that can take over a person's life and prevent their accomplishing things that are more worth while.

Feats of extreme self-denial and austere living, then, do not as such demonstrate temperance – it all depends on the soundness of the judgement that underlies and sustains the self-denial. Misers, for example, live most austerely, but not because they are devoting their lives to particularly worthwhile pursuits that require self-denial. On the other hand, it may be that temperance does require of us extreme self-denial – it would appear to do so, for example, if in truth all bodily indulgences are hazardous and liable to unhinge our critical powers. And we should perhaps expect those who believe in both original sin and an after-life to support Plato's repudiation of all but the 'necessary pleasures' – eating only to avoid the distractions of hunger or infirmity etc. – rather than to approve Aristotle's openness to the possibility of innocuous, moderate self-indulgence.

Let us proceed on the assumption that temperance is compatible with a modicum of 'good living'. In that case, have we any good reason to regard business life as especially difficult to reconcile with living temperately? As we have already noted, a great many managers are busy making money for *others*: they are not owner–managers. If they are making money it is on other people's behalf and, as we have also noted, how the beneficiaries of the service provided by managers spend their dividends, whether on frivolous living, is hardly the managers' responsibility.

There may, though, be certain types of business activity that do tend to undermine temperance. We have remarked that while riches may put a strain on temperance, riches are not peculiar to business life – nor, we should add, are riches achieved by all who are successful in business. But sudden fluctuations of fortune as opposed to a steady increase of income may be characteristic of certain types of business life and may put a special strain on the virtue. Then again, in some lines of business, executives are obliged to live ostentatiously so as to maintain for their firms an image of successfulness. Thus a business man who might be perfectly content to drive to work in a Mini may be prevailed upon to drive a Rolls. Yet once a person gets used to luxurious living, it may become difficult to revert to simpler living, for example on retirement.

As a matter of fact, though, it seems that many people who are outstandingly successful in money making live exceptionally abstemious lives: if they lack temperance it is more likely because they are *too* abstemious, their intemperance involves unreasonable self-denial – unreasonable, because the money making dominates their lives at the expense of living well. Such people, it seems, are interested neither in money making as such nor in money spending. Maybe they are dominated by the desire to win – or anyway, by the desire not to lose. Ivan Boesky seems to have been such a person, according to his wife, Seema. Recall her comments (quoted in chapter 4) in an interview with Barbara Walters for the American ABC network's *20/20* programme, on how he would work 'around the clock, seven days a week'. For what did he do it? In the same interview, Seema Boesky recalled that when, in 1982, *Forbes* magazine first listed Boesky among the wealthiest people in the US, he was upset. She had assumed that he disliked the publicity, and made some remark to that effect. Boesky replied: 'That's not what's upsetting me. We're no-one. We're nowhere. We're at the bottom of the list and I promise you that I won't shame you like that again ever. We will not remain at the bottom of that list.'[21] As Peter Singer observes, 'The craving to win, whether in business or in sport, is the modern version of the labours of Sisyphus – a sentence to never-ending labour without a goal.'[22]

It may be thought that many people in business who are not personally unduly worldly are none the less implicated in encouraging excessive worldliness, hence intemperance, in others. Now, the connection between being temperate oneself and having a secondary concern that other people be temperate is not at all obvious – if it even exists: unlike the connection between being just oneself and caring that others be just. All the same, is it not implausible to suppose that individuals who are themselves temperate, who therefore deplore undue worldliness and who are sensitive to the risks of bodily or worldly self-indulgences, should at the same time relish an occupation that is single-mindedly dedicated to promoting consumerism, hence intemperance?

But to what extent is marketing engaged in undermining people's temperance? Marketeers may be accused of deliberately creating in customers 'unnatural' desires so as to sell the products that these desires establish a market for. And in so far as few of our desires qualify as natural – only, F.A. von Hayek suggests,[23] the desires for food, for shelter, for sex – it would seem to be true that most products being marketed are artificial. But, as Hayek proceeds to argue, many artificial products enhance our lives and acquiring a taste for them is an important part of becoming civilized and educated. Thus, there is no reason why the temperate who are in trade should have qualms about selling their products merely because the taste for them has to be acquired. What matters, rather, is whether once such a taste is acquired, it can be kept within bounds so as not to distract us from the other good things in life.

In any case, are not many products on the market genuinely labour saving – they free those who buy them from some of the daily grind of worldly concerns – for example, washing machines and refrigerators. As we have already noted, whether customers use their extra freedom frivolously or not is not the sellers' responsibility. In short, we should expect those who are temperate and who engage in business to be fastidious about the products they promote. But though this implies that they are restricted somewhat in what they market and how they market it, this by no means debars them from successful and satisfying careers in marketing.

Reconciling Careers in Business or in Professions with Having Virtues

It is true that those who have virtues are constrained in particular ways that debar them from seizing on certain opportunities of which less scrupulous persons would take advantage – the just do not lie or cheat; the compassionate reject plans that they foresee will precipitate other people into financial ruin; the temperate reject promotions of products that encourage dangerous addiction.

But there is no reason to suppose that these constraints are not equally restrictive for people not in business who have these virtues, for professionals, for example, in medicine or education: giving patients or students honest appraisals of their state of progress and prospects takes up much more time than does giving glib reassurances – time that could be spent on other patients or students.

The notion, then, that 'business ethics' is peculiarly risible, unlike, say, 'medical ethics', is sheer prejudice. Maybe people think that just because medicine is a caring profession – committed to pursuing duties of humanity – it is to be expected that those who are in medicine are committed to acting in accordance with the virtues. We should not, though, confuse the goal of a practice with the purpose(s) of its practitioners.[24] The goal of commercial business may be simply to make profit for the shareholders. But people who are in business are motivated on the job by various purposes – including, as with medical practitioners, the aim to make a living. And GPs, for example, may be no less vulnerable to the temptations of avarice than are salesmen – some may succumb to lucrative offers from pharmaceutical companies in return for enlisting patients as research subjects in trials that are of doubtful value. Moreover, the fact that the aim of a practice is morally impeccable may itself lull practitioners into engaging in morally indefensible procedures, into assuming too casually that the noble end justifies the dubious means. Only consider what has been done in this century in the name of medical research – quite apart from what went on in Nazi Germany.[25]

Further Reading

On competitiveness in business: the ethical implications
See Sorell and Hendry, *Business Ethics*, chapter 6; Hamel, Doz and Prahalad, 'Collaborate with your competitors'.

On reconciling virtues with business imperatives
See Cuilla, 'Business ethics'; Nash, *Good Intentions Aside*; Solomon, *Ethics and Excellence*; Sternberg, *Just Business*, chapter 3 and pp. 105–7 of chapter 4.

On honesty and on honesty in business
See Sissela Bok, *Lying*; Carr, 'Is business bluffing ethical?'; Jackson, 'Honesty in marketing'.

Study Questions

1   'Advertising which highlights the flaws or failures of the competition is moral [not unethical] so long as it is accurate.'[26]
    Do you agree? Is engaging in this type of advertising incompatible with a virtue? If so, which?

2   'Cunning deception and concealment of one's strengths and intentions, not kindness and open-heartedness, are vital in poker. No-one thinks any the worse of poker on that account. And no-one should think any the worse of the game of business because its standards of right and wrong differ from the prevailing traditions of morality in our society.'[27]
    How appropriate is this analogy? On this, see Solomon.[28]

3   Peter Geach[29] sums up the virtue of temperance as a hum-drum matter of common sense. Do you agree? Does it, in your view, require moderation in indulgence or abstinence? Justify your answer.

7

Role Duties

Finding Our Bearings

The aim of this book is to clarify what practices and policies in business are ethically defensible. The aim is to work out a map of morality, so to speak, that helps people in business to find a right track – *a* right track not *the* right track – a right track being any track that avoids wrongdoing and allows acting well. Thus, we have marked off certain areas as no-go or danger areas and we have also indicated points of continuing interest, which those who have virtues (because of their concerns) keep within reach of. So far we have been reflecting on what is ethically defensible or indefensible for *any* of us to do, in business or not in business, whoever and wherever we are: the virtues are the same for everyone and we all need to uphold the constraints on force and fraud that enable us to live in peace. But there is more to morality and to what avoiding wrongdoing and acting well imports for each of us individually. We find ourselves in certain roles – what particular roles varies from person to person. The roles we have or take on carry with them specific duties and concerns. These modify what it is ethically defensible for us to do.

How Roles Modify what Is Ethically Defensible

Roles modify what it is ethically defensible for you to do in two ways:

1   By *adding* extra restrictions to what you may do: if you are the chauffeur, you must not drink; if you are the consultant, you must not gossip.

2   By *releasing* you from what is otherwise not defensible for you to do: normally it is wrong to lie, but as an investigating detective or journalist, you may 'need' to lie.

Notoriously, the requirements of a role do not automatically justify. If a role requires that you do what is otherwise wrong, does that indicate that the role itself is indefensible? Suppose, for example, that the role requires that you lie and this is even foreseeable, a routine necessity – as with the role of the thief, but also with that of the undercover investigator. We have already noted that not all lies are equally serious, that there are circumstances where lying can be justified. Now, while it is not enough to justify doing what is otherwise indefensible simply by pointing out that a role you have necessitates it, aren't there some roles that in some circumstances will justify some lies?

Consider, for example, the predicament doctors face when comforting bereaved families, if the families ask, as they sometimes do, whether *they* could have done anything to have prevented the untimely death – whether if they had called the doctor sooner. . . . Doctors in such circumstances may unhesitatingly lie and advise their trainee doctors to do likewise: 'Why add to their feelings of guilt and misery, even if in fact they probably might have prevented the tragedy had they acted differently?' If doctors are justified in lying in these circumstances, if they see it as part of their duty to the bereaved to do so, it will be because in the circumstances, the lying is not an abuse of trust or is not a serious abuse of trust. But whether doctors are justified in lying to patients or their relatives in *other* circumstances needs to be examined case by case. It is never sufficient simply to point out that a lie is useful or necessary in relation to the duties or concerns of a role you occupy.

In other words, it is not enough to justify your lying, that unless you lie, you will not succeed in your purpose – even if the purpose is dictated by your role and is in itself noble or, at any rate, innocent. All the same, there may be more you can say in defence of your lying in pursuance of some role or purpose in regard to the particular circumstances. You are being interviewed for a post and you are asked about some aspect of your private life that is irrelevant to your suitability for the post and which you wish to keep private: is a lie in such a case an abuse of trust? If it is, is it a serious abuse?

Problems and Dilemmas

In chapter 3, we drew a distinction between two types of hard choice: problems and dilemmas. You have a problem, where the choice you are making is between alternatives where whichever you do will not be wrong, but moral considerations may tell in favour of one rather than the other. You have a dilemma, where the choice you face is between alternatives each of which *seems* to involve doing what is wrong. We noted that whereas in a game like chess there are no dilemmas – because the regulatory rules do not conflict and always have priority over the guideline rules – in life we do sometimes find ourselves in situations where the regulatory rules of morality seem to conflict, and also in situations where a regulatory rule seems to be overridden by other moral considerations.

In other words, the regulatory rules of morality do not have the same kind of clear-cut, uncomplicated authority as the rules of chess have. Promises are regulatory – they act as constraints on our freedom of choice: if you have promised to sell this car to me at a certain price, you are bound not to sell it to someone else or to up the price on me. Yet that is not to say that you are never justified in failing to keep a promise it is in your power to keep. Promises can conflict with each other. You may accidentally have promised the same car to two customers. You may have promised in good faith to have this car ready for me to collect today but now renege on that promise because there has been a burglary overnight on the premises and for the time being you have more pressing immediate duties, talking to the police and comforting the beaten-up nightwatchman. Note that in this last case, you would be setting aside your promise to me, not in order to fulfil a promise to someone else, nor on account of some other constraint-type duty but out of a concern that is legitimate and in the situation of overriding importance.

I have suggested[1] that moral dilemmas must be resolvable: if one is to make sense of morality, its commands cannot oblige us to do the impossible. It cannot really be our duty to do x and not to do x. Since it is always possible for promises to conflict with each other, we do not regard promises as all equally binding: we distinguish between our prima facie duties and our actual duties. Prima facie, it may be your duty to do x and your duty not to do x. But actually it cannot be your duty to do and not to do. Suppose that you discover to your dismay that you have promised to represent your company at an important meeting and that this conflicts with your commitment to attend your daughter's graduation. Your fault entirely, perhaps – but that is by the by. The point is that you cannot *keep* both promises. Which in the circumstances is more important might not be obvious (your daughter and your boss may not agree), but the dilemma is in principle resolvable – no one would insist that every promise is equally binding.

If you have promised to do and not to do, you have a dilemma – resolvable, as we have noted. But suppose that you have not promised, but that you are being pressed – on the one hand, by your daughter, to attend her graduation, and on the other hand, by your boss, to represent the company at a meeting which, you see, coincides with the graduation. In this case you are not *obliged* to do as either requests: they are presenting you with a problem rather than a dilemma. Typically, competing claims do not give rise to dilemmas. They do not present you with an either/or where each alternative open to you appears to be wrong. In the case of competing claims, you have to choose between alternatives, each of which has a drawback: each alternative prevents your acting on a role-related concern in a particular way. But the duties to which such concerns give rise tend to be open-ended and non-dischargeable type duties where you have discretion over how and when you act on them. Thus is it possible to accommodate competing claims.

Competing Claims

Given that we all occupy various roles, problems of this kind are unavoidable. The parent with young children seeks a balance between competing claims of work and home. That one role limits your ability to pursue another does not mean that the roles are incompatible. The roles are compatible so long as a reasonable balance can be struck. The demands of a role, obviously, may change in a way that renders it no longer possible to strike a reasonable balance – as if you can no longer cope with your job because your child has been permanently disabled by accident or illness.

The requirements of a role may change in such a way as to render it no longer compatible with one's other moral concerns, whether or not these are role-related. You may decide to give up your job in a publishing firm when it branches out into selling hard porn. You may not be able to reconcile your role in promoting this material with social attitudes and practices that you think need protecting. Of course, if you have such a concern it need not fall within the ambit of this or that role you have. It may be simply a virtue-related concern. We have seen how these concerns are appropriate for any human being to have. And, being a human being is not as such pursuing a role.

A role may be innocent in itself yet necessitate that you set aside a moral constraint in a particular situation – which may be one-off or a regular occurrence. Doing business in some countries may necessitate turning a blind eye to kick-backs. If that is so, if you cannot compete unless you do it *their* way, does that mean that you must give up doing business there, or can you argue that the necessity justifies? The necessity is never enough to justify what is otherwise wrong. Further argument is needed, to establish that the wrong in the circumstances is relatively unimportant and that the alternative involves significant sacrifice.

Indeed, we ought to be wary of appeals to one's role to justify what would otherwise be wrong, for two reasons:

1   The necessity must be real.
2   There must be more to the justification than simply the role-necessity.

The necessity must be real. But we know that people will claim that they *have to* do something where we can see that is not so – as, where they have discretion and should be exercising it in the case in hand. There has to be more to the justification than the mere role-related necessity. If the role requires that you do something that is otherwise wrong, it is never enough to argue that you have to because of the role. To justify treating the role-necessity as a moral necessity, you have to explain why in the circumstances you are not rather obliged to step out of the role.

Roles in Business

Dilemmas and problems crop up independently of the roles we have. Here, though, we are particularly interested in the roles people have in business and how these bear on what it is ethically defensible for people to do in their business roles. But, maybe, we should not suppose that everyone working *for* a business is *in* business. If you are in business, you have a particular role in relation to the aims of that business and you will have an interest in pursuing that role so as to advance its contribution to the underlying aim. If you are working for a business, you do not necessarily have any reason to support the underlying aim that defines the service you provide. If you are a telephonist working in a business that is run on cooperative principles – like the John Lewis Partnership[2] – then you are in the business, concerned to further its underlying aim. If you are a telephonist working for a business that is not a cooperative, why should you care about how the business you work for fares? You want to keep your job and to that extent your interests are bound up with those of the business but you may not care, nor have reason to care, if it prospers – if it does, there may be no reason to expect the benefits to trickle down to you.

Jill, let us suppose, is a telephonist working for a travel agency. She arrives at work early one morning and happens to overhear a senior member of the agency talking on the telephone. She realizes that this person is selling confidential information to some-one outside. Does she have a duty to report this? If she does not, is she failing in loyalty? Is she a *party* to the dishonesty since she could put a stop to it and does not? Does it not make a differ-ence whether she is in the business or merely working for the busi-ness? Suppose the person who overhears is not a telephonist but the office cleaner. The office cleaner surely is *not* in the business

– more obviously not, perhaps, than the telephonist. To be sure, your duties in a job are not confined to obeying the law. And your duties as a *member* of a business firm might actually explicitly include furthering the business aim – hence, protecting the business against damaging leaks. Your duties working *for* a business may not warrant any such overall commitment. You do your job conscientiously – it does not include reporting on disloyal staff. If you are just, as we have noted, you do have a secondary concern that justice be done. You will not, then, be indifferent to instances of disloyalty that you encounter. All the same, you are not obliged, because you care about justice, to prevent injustices whenever you can.

Suppose, though, that you are a member of the business firm – are *in* the business, so to speak – must you then report damaging leaks made by colleagues in the firm? You have an obligation to promote the firm's prosperity, and damaging leaks damage. All the same, your obligation to promote the firm's prosperity is an ongoing open-ended type of obligation. It does not dictate that you report this incident and your deciding not to does not necessarily demonstrate a lack of the concern your role commits you to. Suppose, for example, that the colleague who is leaking information is in financial difficulties and hitherto has worked honestly and diligently for the firm. If you report the incident he will be sacked. You might decide instead to caution him, to rearrange staff duties so that he is not privy to confidential matters of importance and to persuade him to seek counselling. There might be some risks involved in following this course. But your obligation to the business you are in need not preclude your taking risks. After all, if on holiday, you go skiing, although this might result in your being laid off work for a while with a broken leg, no one supposes on that account that you are failing in your duties to the firm.

Compromise and Obligation

Is it always unethical to compromise where one is under obligation? The very notion of obligation indicates necessity – what *must* be done/avoided. How, then, can we in the same breath insist that an action is necessary (obligatory) *and* that compromise over doing it is permissible? But what is obligatory often does not dictate (or preclude) a specific course of action in a given situation. Especially is this true in respect of obligations of the open-ended, non-dischargeable type – for example, the obligation to educate your children – or yourself. Assuming that you are under such an obligation, you are not therefore obliged to seize every opportunity that arises to do so. The fact that right now you are not energetic in this regard although you could be (you are not, as it happens, occupied with other overriding obligations) does not show that you are *compromising* over this particular obligation. You may be reasonably zealous and mindful of this obligation even so. To ascertain whether you are, we would need to survey how in general it influences your choices and attitudes – for example, whether you are wont to pass up opportunities casually and to the evident detriment of your children's education.

Obligations necessarily qualify one another – as Cordelia reminds her sisters when they protest their duty to their father to be unqualified although both are married women: 'Why have my sisters husbands, if they say, they love you all? Haply, when I shall wed, that lord, whose hand must take my plight, shall carry half my love with him, half my care, and duty: sure, I shall never marry like my sisters, to love my father all.'[3] Obligations of the non-dischargeable type – such as that owed by children to their parents – allow scope for discrimination over how and when we act on them. This makes it possible for us to accommodate our other obligations and our own legitimate needs and interests.

Obligations of the constraint type – such as the obligations not to lie, cheat and break promises – are more strictly binding. They rule out certain means to whatever ends we happen to be pursuing. But, as we have already noted, we do not regard such obligations as all equally strictly binding. We expect to encounter difficulties over the promises we make and to be justified in breaking promises sometimes – as when it turns out that one promise can only be kept by breaking another. But in such circumstances, assuming that we judge reasonably which promise to honour, we are not in breaking the other promise compromising on what we owe: in the circumstances, the promise we break is one we are not now obliged to keep. The person to whom the promise was made has not been wronged. Thus, it need not tell against my virtue that I break a promise to you on a particular occasion.

But what if I cheat you or lie to you? Don't we need to treat the obligations not to lie and not to cheat as more strictly binding? The most conscientious among us sometimes have to break a promise, but we do not expect to find those who are conscientious 'having' to cheat or lie on occasion – or do we? Were not adolescents arriving at Nazi concentration camps justified in lying about their age so as to get included with the adults and sent to work rather than be sent to the gas chambers with the children? But can one extend the justification to circumstances that are not so unusual: is a single mother justified in lying to social security if that is the only way she can obtain enough money to provide a decent living for herself and her family? In this case we would probably want to enquire, (1) whether the alleged necessity is real – that there is no other way – and (2) what is being deemed to be a 'decent' living.

The bindingness of constraint-type obligations seems to vary between types of obligation: we expect honest people to 'have to' break promises on occasion and to do so with a clear conscience as we, maybe, do not normally expect honest people to cheat or lie on occasion with a clear conscience. But the bindingness of particular constraint-type obligations also varies according to circumstances: we do not regard all sorts of promises as equally overridable nor all kinds of lies as equally serious. Cheating someone of a penny is less serious than cheating someone of a pound – and that, less serious than cheating someone of their last pound. An honest person may judge that the standards of honesty that should be applied vary from one context to another: that it is necessary in some contexts to have very strict standards – for example, when negotiating a contract – and not at all necessary in certain other contexts – for example, contexts where trust is not needed, as when passing the time in casual chit-chat with strangers while waiting in a queue.

Ethics Applied to Case Studies

We need a map just where finding an ethically suitable track is difficult – where we do not agree with one another as to what is a suitable track. In the study of business ethics, case studies are used to represent some of the kinds of problems and dilemmas people in business find themselves up against. What has ethics to offer as a resource for analysing these cases? Can it provide a framework or criterion for distinguishing suitable from unsuitable tracks?

The two common approaches that are regularly scouted, utilitarian and deontological, are both theoretically flawed (as I shall explain in the next chapter) and practically unsatisfactory. One respect in which the utilitarian approach is practically unsatisfactory is that it is too yielding towards role-related necessities; the deontologist approach, on the other hand, may be too unyielding. As the deontological approach is often characterized rather loosely to cover a range of views having in common nothing more than their rejection of the utilitarian approach, it is easy to think that one has to jump one way or the other. But this is not so.

Utilitarians will, I suggest, readily – too readily – allow necessities to determine what is a suitable track: they will consider the details of the case in hand – all factors that bear on what will result in net benefit. Quite simply, whatever is necessary for achieving net benefit is justified. Utilitarians will not see any value in the distinction drawn here between dilemmas and problems. They will lump both types of hard choice together because they do not recognize the importance of boundary-setting constraint-type duties within which we may pursue our purposes and act on our roles. Some utilitarians do allow special weight to attach to such duties but where they constrict choice aimed at net benefit, such constraints are immediately swept aside.

Deontologists, on the other hand, take the constraint-type duties too seriously. They treat them as analogous to the regulatory rules of chess: never to be set aside because that is necessary to achieve some significant good. I suggest a third way here. We should agree with the deontologists that role- or purpose-related necessity is never by itself enough to justify setting aside a constraint-type duty, but allow that necessity taken together with other considerations can on occasion justify setting aside a constraint.

It is difficult to see the possibility of a third way here because once one allows necessity to be relevant, it is easy to suppose it is decisive – though, of course, that does not follow. Because we allow necessity to be relevant, we need not yield to any and every necessity: should not, for example, in the case of Brendan Power of the Life Insurance Association, who is reported to say, 'We should tell our clients that business is great and that we really are busy.' He goes on to observe that, 'Initially it does not matter whether it is true or not.' Why does it not matter? Because, of course, the lie is necessary: 'It is vital for our success that we eliminate all negative words and phrases from our vocabulary and, equally important, that we replace them with positive ones.'[4]

The third way that I am recommending is neither utilitarian nor deontological, although it treats duties, rights and utilities as all relevant to how dilemmas and problems should be resolved. The third way relies on the judgement of those who have virtues, for resolving particular dilemmas and problems. The honest person, I suggest, does not treat lies as mere drawbacks to be weighed against benefits: the honest person does not consider lying as a possible solution except where there is more to be said than that a lie is necessary to achieve a desirable result. On the other hand, someone who is honest may still be prepared to lie on occasion, special occasion, taking account of other additional factors, not just that the lie is a necessary means to a desirable end.

Further Reading

On roles
See Emmet, *Rules, Roles and Relations.*

On dilemmas
See Gowans, *Moral Dilemmas.*

Study Questions

1 'The loyal corporate representative insists on proper returns for the shareholders and holds the corporation accountable for its performance in achieving them. Thus shareholders and directors, managers and employees are being loyal, not disloyal, when they

criticise bad management and errant directors: it is to the corporate purpose, not the current administration, management, or format of the enterprise that loyalty is due.'[5]

Do you agree? In what circumstances do you consider whistle-blowing to be consistent with loyalty; in what, inconsistent?

2   Consider the distinction drawn in this chapter between those who are working *in* a business and those who are working for a business. Do you see this distinction as relevant to what is owed in loyalty at work?

3   Consider the distinction drawn in this chapter between problems and dilemmas, then read the following two cases. How would you classify each: as a problem or as a dilemma? Why?

    i   'I worked in the office of a company that distributed spare parts for heavy machinery throughout northern Michigan. When somebody would call in for a part, we would look up the number, price, and inventory level on the computer. The boss told us always to say that we had the part in stock, even if the inventory level showed us that we were out, that we didn't have any left. His argument was that we could always get the part from Chicago in a day or two and that a day or two was not going to hurt anyone. I didn't like it because it meant I had to lie to somebody about once a day.'[6]

    ii   'I was working for a company that supplied packaging materials throughout Ohio. It was just a sales job, but there was a good commission structure, so I could make a lot of money if I was successful. Packaging materials are close to a commodity. You can buy the same boxes and fillers and tape from just about anyone, at just about the same price. The suppliers tend to compete on service to the customer and on gifts to the purchasing agent. Not all of the purchasing agents are the same, but many of them will tell you exactly what they want: a new TV for their rec room, a pair of tickets to a ball game, a set of tires for their car. You either give them what they want, or you don't get the order.'[7]

4   'Saudi Arabian contracts worth almost £900 m are in sight for British companies after the government's decision to expel Mohammed Masari, the Saudi dissident based in north London.'[8]

Did the necessity of expelling Masari so as to persuade the Saudis to lift their ban on new orders from British companies present the British government with a problem or a dilemma? Was the decision to expel Masari justified?

8

Good Practice in Business

What Is Good Practice in Business?

Good practice, ethically defensible practice, we understand to involve both practice that avoids doing wrong (injustice) and that is consistent with the virtues generally (that is to say, the virtues other than justice). We have considered the kinds of dilemmas and problems that can make it difficult to identify what is good practice – how different constraint-type obligations we are under as a matter of avoiding doing wrong can appear to conflict; how occasionally it seems defensible to set aside a constraint-type obligation in order to achieve some important end – though we reject the idea that necessity automatically justifies – how even where the alternatives we are choosing between are both within the realm of the morally permissible, it may be difficult to judge which is more appropriate in relation to morally significant concerns (namely, concerns that those who have virtues have).

How, then, can the study of ethics (by which, it will be remembered,[1] we mean not a study of what people *think* is ethically defensible but of what actually *is* ethically defensible) help us to think well when faced with actual moral dilemmas and problems in business? The study of business ethics alongside that of medical ethics and other branches of applied ethics has taken root over the past 20 years or so. Typically, attempts to apply ethics in this or that field have drawn on utilitarian theory or deontological theory, or a bit of both. I have already claimed that these approaches are unsatisfactory both as ethical theories and as sources of practical guidelines to apply to dilemmas or problems. I will now explain why – but briefly, since what I have to say against these approaches is nothing new. Yet people continue to try to apply them, maybe despite acknowledged flaws and because they see no clear alternative. I will first indicate what each approach involves, then I will indicate their theoretical weaknesses. Next, I will illustrate the practical unsatisfactoriness of these approaches by applying them to a test case. Finally, I will discuss how our own virtues theory applies to the test case.

Utilitarianism

The account I give here of utilitarianism is brief and brisk. There are many thoughtful, sophisticated studies and defences and different versions. It is not to our purpose here to delve into all of these: some pointers are given in the further reading at the end of this chapter. What is common to all is the claim that morality is about doing good and that in assessing the morality of what we choose to do, we should be considering simply and solely the utility of acting this way or that. Thus, it is sometimes described as an 'outcome morality' – since the critical question utilitarians ask about alternatives under consideration is: what will be the outcome of doing this or that? What one ought to do is always what produces the better outcome – more utility.

If this theory is to be of practical use, explanation must be forthcoming as to what counts as a good or bad consequence: we cannot measure the utility of various alternatives until we know what we mean by utility. Secondly, we need to know to whom morality requires us to do good – how far we need to expand the circle of concern so as to include all those, and only those, whose good matters. There are, no doubt, further questions to raise just to clarify what utilitarianism amounts to, but let us stick to these. We ask: (1) what is good? and (2) whose good matters?

To both of these questions different utilitarians give different answers. Alternative answers to the first question include: pleasure, happiness, welfare and the satisfaction of preferences. Alternative answers to the second question include: oneself, mankind, all sentients, all sentients alive now or who will live in the future.

We do not need to go further to notice that applying this theory – whichever answers are selected – has its problems. How feasible is it to compare and calculate alternatives in the way that the theory demands? We need a 'utilometer', but there is no such thing. The difficulty of doing the calculation is more obvious the more individuals we have to take into our calculation. On the other hand, any drawing of the circle that excludes some may seem arbitrary and impossible to defend.

Still, if the theory were convincing as a theory we might stand by it, notwithstanding the difficulty of applying it. After all, the difficulty of applying it could just reflect a fact of life: if the aim of morality is to maximize good, we should expect that our success in selecting correctly among the alternatives open to us will be very limited, given our lack of knowledge, the unpredictability of things and our own deficient moral motivation. Is it, though, a credible theory if it imposes on us a pervasive and unrelenting obligation to maximize utility? The implications of this seem to run counter to many of the assumptions of traditional Western morality (I mean, to assumptions that are common to the ethics of Judaeo-Christian ethics, Muslim ethics and also the ethics of Plato and Aristotle). So much the worse for tradition, the utilitarian may say – though in fact utilitarians usually take pains to demonstrate that their theory, properly interpreted, does not go against tradition in any significant way. But before we chuck views about morality that are deep-rooted and arguably have stood the test of time, we want to have confidence that the theory we convert to has compensating strengths: if practically awkward, is it theoretically, at least, sound? Does it stand up as a theory?

I suggest that it does not. It fails to make sense of the language of obligation, of the 'moral must'. It fails, that is, to answer the question we examined in chapter 4: what reason you or I have to act for moral reasons. If the aim of morality is to maximize happiness – whoever's – or preference-satisfactions, why should you or I do that? What does it matter, to you or me? Assume that you and I are clear-headed and fully informed of any relevant matters; what reason do we have to do what morality asks of us, to make its aim our aim, indeed our first aim? Never mind the question of whether morality so conceived, requiring us to maximize utility, isn't preposterously demanding. My question is, can we even make sense of the importance to each of us individually as agents of taking on this aim – how does it connect with anything we care about or need to care about? Surely, any theory of morality should at least explain why morality matters, why we mind about each other's morality, why we are, and need to be, intolerant of injustice.

Deontological Theory: What it is Against

The term 'deontological' derives from two Greek words: *deon*, meaning 'duty', and *logos*, meaning 'account' or 'study'. It has crept into writings on applied ethics and is hardly to be found in the writings of philosophers elsewhere. As we have already remarked, the term is not well-defined, and those who call themselves deontologists may have nothing more in common than their repudiation of utilitarianism. Perhaps, we can add that they share what is their main objection to utilitarianism – that it fails to make sense of the importance of matters of justice. I have argued that utilitarianism attaches overriding importance to the moral aim but fails to explain that importance. Deontologists complain that utilitarians, by tying the moral aim to maximizing utility, fail to explain the importance within morality of considerations of justice. We have noted how avoiding wrong doing involves observing certain constraints – duties that set the boundaries within which we pursue our lives, like the regulatory rules of games. While utilitarians can agree that such rules have moral importance – our lives would be less happy if we did not recognize and respect these constraints – deontologists note how easily a utilitarian will allow such constraints to be set aside or modified. After all, the basic moral aim is to maximize utility and while in general observing the rules of justice contributes to that goal, there are bound to be many excep-tions; it is always, in principle, in order to ask whether it is not necessary to set aside or modify the rule. And the answer the utilitarian gives is, 'If departing from the rule (or changing it) will yield a better outcome (more utility) all things considered, then departing from the rule is necessary – is morally obligatory'.

Thus, utilitarians will too readily allow a necessity in relation to a utility-producing goal to override the constraint-type duties.

Whereas we have distinguished here between hard choices that are problems and hard choices that pose dilemmas, that distinction will seem uninteresting to the utilitarian; it will have no practical relevance. The utilitarian will lump together all types of hard choices and resolve them simply by seeking a balance between competing considerations – a balance that promises to yield the best outcome. Deontologists object to this cavalier balancing of considerations because it down-plays the regulatory-type function of certain moral considerations. The duty not to lie, they will say, is not just a drawback, to be weighed in the balance. It is unlike the duty, say, to promote justice in the world. This latter duty is of a different kind. It is an ongoing non-dischargeable kind, allowing one discretion over how one acts on it. Whether to act on it in this way or that is properly something one weighs up, considering pros and cons.

Bernard Williams famously sketched two scenarios in which it seems that from a utilitarian perspective it is obvious and easy to see what one should do but where many people would feel that even if they agreed with the action that utilitarians would approve, they would have difficulties over this choice – difficulties which hardly make sense to utilitarians.[2] One of the scenarios concerns an out-of-work chemist who is offered a job to work in an establishment doing research in chemical and biological warfare. The chemist is against such research establishments, for moral reasons, but he needs the job and if he does not take it, someone else will. The deontologist understands this to be an issue of principle. Where a principle is at stake it makes sense to refuse to think consequentially. 'To have no principles' is just to be the sort of person who is prepared to do anything if in the circumstances it yields better results. The utilitarian is primarily concerned with results, only secondarily with how they are achieved – by whom and by what means. Thus, from a utilitarian view, the argument, 'If you don't do it, others will' is morally relevant – it tells in favour of your doing it yourself. But that kind of justification seems alien to the attitude of someone who has principles. The person of principle rejects certain types of actions, quite simply, 'because they are wrong'.

So far, in finding fault with the utilitarians, I am in agreement with the deontologists. It is when they go on to offer an alternative theory to apply to dilemmas and problems that I suggest we should part company. But since there is no well-defined theory of deontology corresponding to utilitarian theory,[3] it is difficult, especially in keeping with our aim here to be brief and brisk, to be fair. It is much easier to say what deontologists are against than to say what they are for. They are against accounts of morality that do not give due weight to duties, rights and principles.

Deontological Theory: What it is For

Here, let us examine one very common and influential deontological approach, Kantianism, based on the ethics of Immanuel Kant (1724–1804). Contemporary Kantians especially fasten on to Kant's idea that people are owed respect: that they are never to be treated as mere means to other people's ends. Kantians take this to be the expression of an important insight. But what exactly does it mean – treat people never merely as means? If people are owed respect, what exactly is it about people that entitles them to respect? Respect is paid to a person in regard to this or that – their skill in bowling, their social tact, their courage in the face of adversity. The idea that everyone is owed respect because they are human beings does not make obvious sense. Respect is owed, if it is, in respect of something. How is simply being human a basis for respect – aside, anyway, from a theological standpoint according to which humans are created by God and for that reason to be treated with respect? There is a story that in the 1930s, when it became known that Richard Strauss had accepted the appointment to conduct at Bayreuth, Toscannini, who had refused to set foot in Germany so long as Nazi persecution of Jews continued, was asked by a reporter what he thought of Richard Strauss. He responded: 'When I think of Richard Strauss the musician, I take my hat off. When I think of Richard Strauss, the man, I put it back on.'

Here, then, is a way of understanding the notion of respect for a person – as respect for their qualities of moral character. Toscannini, according to the story, evidently thought Strauss to have shown a moral failing in agreeing to take on such a position in Bayreuth when Jewish musicians were being expelled from orchestras. But this is not how Kantians understand the notion of respect – since they hold that every human being is owed equal respect whereas on the above account individuals would only be owed it if they earned it by their exercise of virtues (babies and small children would not be owed it at all).

In fact, it is not easy to make sense of this idea that everyone is owed respect – what it means and why it might be morally of first importance. One way of understanding the injunction to treat people with respect is to take it to mean simply: respect people's moral rights – avoid doing wrong. But if that is all that is being said, while it seems intelligible and important, it does not indicate a theory. Kant does indeed have a theory – an account of rational choice according to which there are compelling reasons for avoiding wrongdoing, which do not depend on what rational agents want or need. But contemporary Kantians tend not to endorse Kant's philosophical underpinnings to his moral theory, although they hang on to his injunction that people are owed respect. Perhaps they dismiss the need to ground what for them is a basic intuition. After all, utilitarians too start from an intuition – though they may not admit it – that utility ought to be maximized.

Another way of understanding the injunction to treat people with respect is to take it to mean that you must never treat people in ways that they do not consent to. Consent, of course, must be real. It is not real if not (adequately) informed and free, and there are well-known difficulties about both of these aspects of consent. But here, perhaps, we do have the outlines of a theory: the basic requirement to avoid wrongdoing is a requirement to treat people only in ways that they consent to. People's moral rights will on this view have to do with the protection against being 'used'; that is, being treated in ways to which they do not consent.

Yet, it is obviously not always wrong to treat people in ways that they do not consent to. People are arrested, tried and put in prison: they do not (usually) consent. Children are compelled to go to school. We are all compelled to pay taxes. 'People must only be treated in ways they consent to' is not a credible account of what avoiding wrongdoing involves. So, it will be said, it is not actual consent that is required but, however you treat people, it must be in a manner that they could consent to in principle – would consent to if they were reasonable. This rescues the credibility of the requirement – but at a price: are we any the wiser now as to what is wrong with wrongdoing? Are we not here simply saying the same thing in other words: you can reasonably object to how you are being treated just when your rights are not being respected: your rights are not being respected just when you can reasonably object to how you are being treated?

All the same, there does seem to be something in the Kantian notion that people are owed respect, something which expresses a fundamental disquiet about utilitarianism – that it does not respect the separateness of persons, as Rawls puts it.[4] It is the notion that lies behind what Willy Loman's wife says of him, in Arthur Miller's *Death of a Salesman*: 'He's not the finest character that ever lived. But he's a human being, and a terrible thing is happening to him. So attention must be paid. He is not to be allowed to fall into his grave like an old dog. Attention, attention must finally be paid to such a person.'[5]

I suggest that there are two virtues that shed light on this notion: justice and humanity. Justice involves giving people their due. What someone is due may depend in part on what they have been, services past, which we in gratitude have a duty to remember and pay attention to. Humanity, as defined here, involves civility based on considerateness and compassionate understanding towards the predicaments of others. From a utilitarian perspective, how you treat someone should be dictated by the utility to be gained by treating them one way or another – past services might not now be relevant. A friend who was useful to you once may now be something of an embarrassment. The utilitarian perspective is incorrigibly forward-looking. Someone who is just (and loyal) does not forget past services; they do not diminish in significance as time goes by. Someone who is compassionate does not measure out the attention to be paid to individuals who are down on their luck, with an eye to the useful indirect consequences that may flow from helping them. From a utilitarian standpoint, Howard, Willy Loman's boss, does right to sack him – he is no longer effective as a salesman. Loman, though, protests at the injustice, the ingratitude, the inhumanity of this treatment: 'You mustn't tell me you've got people to see – I put 34 years into this firm, Howard, and now I can't pay my insurance! You can't eat the orange and throw away the peel – a man is not a piece of fruit!'[6]

Contractarianism

There is, though, a theory of obligation which, it may be said, makes sense of the Kantian notion that everyone is owed equal respect, and of the idea that justice, just dealing, is bound up with consent, and which, moreover, offers clear guidelines for practical application: contractarianism. We have touched on some versions of contractarianism in chapter 4: the account discussed in Plato's *Republic* and the account given by Hobbes. This theory does make sense of the obligatoriness of avoiding wrongdoing and of the importance of avoiding wrongdoing – by basing our moral obligations on the fiction of a social contract. The contractarian appeals to some basic truths about human nature and human needs – to show that unless we can live in peace, our lives are dreadful. The contractarian sets forth the conditions that we need to observe if peace is to be sustainable: we need to be able to trust and be trusted. From this point we can go on to spell out what kinds of actions must not be tolerated and to delineate what space remains for our pursuing our own individual ways without let or hindrance.

From a Kantian standpoint this theory is promising. It acknowledges that in a sense we are all equal – since we are all equally vulnerable in as much as none of us is better off if we cannot live in peace. And if the terms of the contract are worked out impartially, is it not rational for everyone to consent to it – or rather, since the contract is just a fiction, is it not reasonable for us to treat its terms as if binding on everyone, its terms being such as everyone can consent to in principle? Yet this theory has serious defects. I need to live in peace – but peace with whom? With my neighbours? Who counts here as neighbour? What reason have I to make peace with people who can pose no threat to me – people, for example, who have no status or power such as illegal immigrants or gypsies? But do not such people have moral rights even if it so happens they have no power to threaten the peace?

Furthermore, as we noted in chapter 4, the social contract only binds us to avoid what others among whom we live perceive to be morally required. Thus, if you happen to live in a society which accepts slavery, your tolerance of slavery, your involvement perhaps in slave-trading, is not unjust. In short, on this view, whatever is accepted, is acceptable. Morality is simply a matter of the conventions that a given society chooses. Slavery used to be just. Nowadays, it is unjust. Some day it may become just again. Now, maybe, a society that allows slavery is not based on a contract that conforms to the Kantian requirement of impartiality. It would take us too far afield to pursue that question here. Even if my example is a bad one, the point stands, though, that on this view whatever is accepted, consented to, by impartial choosers, is acceptable, is just. Moreover, on this view the essence of injustice is the absence of acceptance, lack of consent. Of course, that is one kind of injustice: the difference between respectable love-making and rape turns precisely on this. But surely there are other kinds of moral wrongdoing that do not turn on this. If Jack kills and eats Jill it hardly serves as an excuse if she has freely and informedly consented to this.

There is a way of getting round these problems. Contractarians may lay down certain ground-rules, 'hypernorms', which must govern the terms of the social contract so as to prevent the contract allowing what some communities might find acceptable but which would still be wrong. The ground-rules might preclude slavery – even if members of a community failed to see its objectionableness. But then the problem arises that the contractarian is relying on rules that are not themselves explained. We are back to intuition.

A Test Case

By way of demonstrating the practical inadequacies of utilitarian and contractarian theories, let us use as a test case one discussed by Sorell and Hendry; the controversial decision by the retailing firm of the John Lewis Partnership, in 1990, to close down one of its London stores, Jones Bros., located in the Holloway area of North London.[7] There were clear commercial reasons for the decision to close down Jones Bros.: the premises, built at the turn of the century, had become inadequate – not enough storage space, expensive to heat and light, and so forth; renovation would have been costly and could not have resolved all these problems and, anyway, the overall company policy was to open large purpose-built department stores outside town centres.

When the decision to close was announced, the local community mounted a campaign to 'Save Jones Bros.'. It protested that the residents in the area had been loyal customers and that many of them – the elderly, for example – would not be able to take up the Company's 'invitation' to shop at other branches of John Lewis. The campaigners wrote, 'By closing Jones Bros., not only will the local community suffer bitterly, but we, as loyal customers, will have no alternative but to think of John Lewis as a company interested solely in maximizing profit, with no concern for inner cities or our loyalty.'

Let us assume for the sake of argument that the commercial case for relocating was sound. Were the campaigners right even so in claiming that John Lewis had obligations to the local community and the loyal customers that should have moved it to save Jones Bros.? Let us notice, first of all, that according to the account of morality set forth in this book, John Lewis was, maybe, not faced with an ethical dilemma – whether or not to close down Jones Bros. – albeit it faced a hard choice. We have defined an ethical (moral) dilemma as a situation where either one has to choose between two prima facie wrongs (like, for example, between breach of confidence and lying) or where one has to choose between setting aside a moral constraint-type obligation or missing an opportunity to achieve an important end. Now the alternatives faced by John Lewis may not fit either description.

I suggest that neither course open to the company involved doing a prima facie wrong. Whichever way it jumped, it would not have been violating anyone's rights. Members of the community who would suffer if the store closed may have felt that they were being treated unfairly – and would doubtless have claimed that they were. But John Lewis should have seen through the protesters' rhetoric. It was no more reasonable for the community to protest that the store was closing down as soon as commercial advantage indicated relocation elsewhere to be advantageous, than it would have been for the store to protest over customers abandoning it for a rival store, had one been established in the community which undercut its prices. After all, even if the community had come to depend on Jones Bros. because it had driven other shops out of the area, it could not have done this single-handedly: it could only have done this because its *customers* chose to abandon the local shops. In so doing, were these fickle customers violating the rights of the local shops? Of course not. Nor, on the other hand, as I shall argue, was John Lewis obliged to go ahead with the closure, given that so doing was commercially advantageous. Management owed owners of the company a reasonable return, not necessarily maximum profits.

Let us now look at our test case from different theoretical perspectives to see how these would apply.

Utilitarian Theory Applied

From a utilitarian perspective, avoiding wrong-doing, the violation of someone's rights, has no special significance. The utilitarian perspective imposes one continuing requirement, to maximize utility. Any choice is wrong, from that perspective, which fails to maximize. Suppose, now, that John Lewis draws on utilitarianism to resolve its hard choice, how will it proceed? As we have noted, there are various versions of utilitarianism, depending on what counts as of utility and whose utility is morally relevant. For our purposes let us suppose that John Lewis identifies utility with the satisfaction of preferences and that it counts any preferences affected by a choice as morally relevant. The company will need, then, to gather information about many people's preferences – not just the preferences of shareholders, employees and suppliers of Jones Bros. but also of their customers and of any other members of the local community who have a preference on the matter. In other words, John Lewis has to weigh up the preferences of all these 'stakeholders', all to whom it matters, or who have a preference, regarding whether or not the shop closes.

But, actually, utilitarianism requires John Lewis to survey preferences even more widely. From a utilitarian perspective, any preferences must be counted in, no matter whose they are. Such an expansive view of whose preferences John Lewis should attend to accords with R. Edward Freeman's account of the scope of responsibility of managers. He says that a business has obligations in respect of all its stakeholders and he defines the stakeholders as, 'any group or individual who can affect, or is affected by, the achievement of a corporation's purpose'.[8] But though Freeman does not mention them, by this definition, members of rival firms whose fortunes may be affected for better or worse depending on how one's own business fares, are stakeholders in one's business. So, according to Freeman's stakeholder theory and to utilitarianism, John Lewis should include in its balancing of preferences the preferences of rival firms. If members of rival firms prefer that John Lewis selects the less profitable alternative, then John Lewis, adopting a utilitarian perspective, ought to count this as a reason why it should choose that alternative – even if the preferences of rival firms are outweighed in the end. Everyone counts for one and no-one for more than one from this perspective. The moral aim is to maximize utility impartially, not favouring one's own firm over others except in so far as a policy of favouring one's own itself yields greater utility overall.

But who seriously thinks that the preferences of employees of rival firms ought to be weighed equally with the preferences of one's own employees? And, anyway, from a moral standpoint, our obligations cannot be determined simply by comparison of future consequences of doing this or that. Obligations relate to what has happened as well as to what might happen depending on how we choose. John Lewis owes special consideration to its members that it does not owe to the world at large – which is not, of course, to say that John Lewis is entitled to ignore altogether the consequences of what it decides for non-members of the company.

Contractarian Theory Applied

Will contractarians see the choice before John Lewis as an ethical dilemma? On the face of it, neither alternative would have involved a breach of contract. There was no contract between Jones Bros. and the local community or its customers. But let us consider the principle behind a policy which permits a shop to close down regardless of cost to the community as soon as closure becomes commercially advantageous. Is this a principle to which a community can consent in principle?

The law may allow business to behave like this. The contractarian, though, does not rely on the happenstance of law to settle the moral defensibility of a policy. Could a community agree to a business setting up, possibly driving out other businesses, on the understanding that the business has no obligation to continue there if doing so ceases to be commercially advantageous? Surely communities can and do consent to businesses operating on this basis. Similarly, a business 'consents' to do business with customers who owe no loyalty to the business, who are within their rights deserting the business and taking their custom elsewhere regardless of the harm that does the business which is abandoned. John Lewis, had it adopted a contractarian perspective, would have viewed the plight of the community if Jones Bros. closed as a moral irrelevance – although it might still have borne importantly on what was now prudent policy for the firm. Given the vigour of the campaign and the sympathetic media hype, it might have become prudent to yield gracefully. But this would not be to concede to the moral claims made out by the protesters, it would simply be to recognize the damage adverse publicity, reasonable or unreasonable, can do a firm.

Our Virtues Theory Applied

Both the above approaches are practically unsatisfactory. The utilitarian approach is unsatisfactory because it is indifferent to rights and claims except in so far as these affect consequences. It requires us to treat all preferences, be they reasonable or unreasonable, friends' or foes', as equally relevant to the sum total of utility that can be achieved. The contractarian approach is practically unsatisfactory in that it dismisses the consequential damage of choices as an irrelevance provided that you are acting on policies to which people could consent in principle. But consequential damage may not be morally irrelevant.

Suppose that you are the chief executive of John Lewis and that it falls to you to advise the Board whether or not it should yield to the campaign against the closure of Jones Bros. If you concede that the closure of this shop will cause significant hardship for some people in the locality, and if you are compassionate (if you have the virtue we are calling humanity), you will see the hardship as a matter of concern and as relevant. You will want to review the issue of whether to close in the light of the points being made by the protesters. You will see the plight of customers who have come to depend on this shop not just as an embarrassment and trouble, but as a problem which you have an obligation to study. You will want to accommodate, if it can be done without serious cost.

You may, though, need to consider not just the possible damage to the company but also the risks for you personally. Suppose that you decide to recommend closure because though you think the cost to the firm of remaining open can be easily absorbed, as, no doubt, the protesters are claiming, you also think that this advice would do your own career no good. If you recommend closure, you are unlikely to be blamed, whatever the outcome of that recommendation being applied. You will be perceived as a strong leader, not yielding to public pressure. If, on the other hand, you persuade the Board to yield to the public pressure, you will get the blame if the consequences are troublesome and in any case you may seem to be less safe and dynamic, less sound.

If such considerations lead you to advise the Board to stick with its planned closure, do you then show yourself to be lacking compassion? Is your recommendation not such as one who has the relevant virtue would make? Not necessarily. We have noted that while having and showing compassion is part of the virtue of humanity, this involves duties of the open-ended non-dischargeable and aspirational sort. You may genuinely care about the plight of customers who have come to depend on Jones Bros. and yet decide not to act on their behalf if it means putting your own career in jeopardy. The customers do not have a right to your exercising your humanity in this way. Similarly, that members of the community allowed local shops to go out of business when they could have supported them, does not show those members to have been deficient in compassion.

In short, whereas the contractarian dismisses the plight of the dependent customers as morally irrelevant, you, as chief executive of John Lewis, if you have the virtue of humanity, will see their plight as relevant. You will see the choice before you not as a dilemma but as a problem, where there are competing concerns to balance – concern for members of the firm you work for (including concern for your own future in the firm – that you are within your rights in taking thought for your own career) and your concern for those in the community who would be seriously adversely affected by closure.

Now it might be objected that you, in your capacity as chief executive, have no business whatsoever allowing sentiments of compassion to intrude on your deliberations over what to advise the Board: your duty to the Board is to advise whichever course will 'maximize long-term owner value'[9] subject only to the constraints that what you advise is in accordance with the law and the requirements of distributive justice and ordinary decency. This is the position argued for by Elaine Sternberg in her account of just (ethically defensible) business. The constraining principles on those who do business, she argues, are just those principles which 'enjoin the basic values without which business as an activity would be impossible'.[10] What are these principles? Business, she argues, 'presupposes conduct which excludes lying, cheating, stealing, killing, coercion, physical violence and most illegality, and instead exhibits honesty and fairness. Taken collectively, these constraints embody the values of what may be called "ordinary decency"'.[11] On her view, then, you would not be free to recommend to the Board just any course of action which did not violate the above principles of ordinary decency, because in your role as chief executive you would be obliged to aim to maximize long-term owner value. You would have no right to be 'nice' to people at the business's expense.

However, this single-minded commitment to the aim of business, which according to Elaine Sternberg is just to maximize long-term owner value by selling goods or services, is, as she points out, not binding on firms which *with the owners' consent* take on other non-business aims. And, of course, many firms are non-profit or are committed to other goals alongside pursuing profits. Managers in such organizations will quite properly seek to balance competing claims or objectives. As a matter of fact, the John Lewis Partnership does take upon itself certain commitments to the community in which it operates. Sorell and Hendry quote from an official company document 'About the John Lewis Partnership' which includes the claim: 'The Partnership . . . very firmly believes that each of its branches owes the duty of a good neighbour to the particular community in which it operates'.[12] But does being a 'good neighbour' commit one to sacrificing commercial gain to prevent one's neighbours suffering hardship? Does being a good neighbour require any more than treating one's neighbours with what Sternberg calls 'ordinary decency'?

All the same, even if the John Lewis Partnership made no pretension to any aims other than to make a profit for its members, acting within the law and with ordinary decency, it still would not necessarily be improper for its chief executive to be moved by compassion to advise against closure. If humanity (as defined here) is a virtue, it should be relevant to all one's dealings. If you, as chief executive of John Lewis, have this virtue, you will not need to seek the Board's permission to exercise it, to be moved by compassion to consider the predicament of the dependent shoppers in relation to the recommendation that you should make. Of course, the concerns of humanity would not justify your lying to the Board or to members of the firm about the advantages and disadvantages of whatever you recommend. But they do justify your taking the predicament of the shoppers into account – with, or without, the members' consent.

In other words, in so far as people in business have a duty to maximize long-term owner value, it is an on-going nondischargeable but discretionary type of duty and its claims on business people should be balanced alongside other claims – claims of family, of friends, and their own legitimate non-business aspirations. If you were the chief executive you would, doubtless, have other claims upon you apart from those arising from your role as chief executive. If you take time off to go to your daughter's graduation, you are not forced to do this by the principles of ordinary decency as defined above, nor is your doing so helpful to the business aim, but that does not make your doing so unethical. The various moral virtues we have seen do involve concerns and these bear on the way those who have these concerns make choices generally. People in business who have these concerns will not see it as their duty to maximize long-term owner value, subject only to the principles of ordinary decency; rather, they may see it as their duty to seek a reasonable return, a reasonable return being one which does not preclude one's having, and acting on, virtue-related concerns.

Further Reading

On utilitarianism
See Smart and Williams, *Utilitarianism: For and Against*: this book contains a full bibliography on utilitarianism; Hare, *Moral Thinking*.

On Kantianism
See O'Neill, *Construction of Reason*; for a Kantian approach to business ethics, see Bowie, *Business Ethics*.

On contractarianism
See Kymlicka, 'The social contract tradition'; for applications to business ethics see Conry, 'A critique of social contracts' and Keeley, 'Continuing the social contract tradition'; see also Donaldson, *The Ethics of International Business*.

Study Questions

1   Robert C. Solomon says that the social responsibility of a corporation 'is not an additional burden on the corporation but part and parcel of its essential concerns, to serve the needs and be fair to not only its investors/owners but those who work for, buy from, sell to, live near or are otherwise affected by the activities that are demanded and rewarded by the free market system'[13]. Comment on this claim from a utilitarian perspective, from a contractarian, from the approach adopted in this book.

2   Consent is at the heart of contractarian theory. You avoid wrong-doing by treating people only in ways they can consent to in principle. But consent, it is said, is not real if not free and informed. What problems, though, might you run into if you were committed to doing business only on these terms – only with the free and informed consent of all parties? Is it a violation of these terms if a company forbids its employees to smoke on the premises?

3   'To analyze business decisions using as a model an individual solely motivated by the maximization of value or of profits, without regard to his or her own character, is totally unrealistic. It does not speak to the role of "nobility," "sacrifice," "sportsman-ship," "heroism," and the like – concepts that motivate real people in resolution of their moral dilemmas.'[14]
Would you expect Elaine Sternberg to dissent from this? If so, why? Would you agree? If not, why not?

9

Good Practice in the Firm

What Counts as Good Practice?

Good practice, we are understanding here to include both avoiding wrongdoing and doing well, acting in a way that is ethically appropriate – that is, consistently with how those who have the virtues would act. Avoiding doing wrong relates to one moral virtue – or, better, group of virtues – which we classify under the heading of 'justice'. These have to do with the constraint-type duties, the regulatory rules of morality. Avoiding wrongdoing involves acting within these constraints. These constraints fix the duties we owe to other people generally – for example, not to use violence against them, not to steal, to lie, or to cheat. Obviously, these constraints are frequently violated and yet we continue to survive as a society. All the same, our living in peace, ability to cooperate – ability, for example, to do business – depends on these constraints being taken seriously and being observed sufficiently generally for it to continue to be rational for us to trust one another.

There are other moral virtues, justice matters aside, that are also essential for our having the best prospect of living well. Living in peace (avoiding anarchy), we have seen to be necessary for living well. But hardly sufficient. We need to have interests and significance in our lives beyond surviving in comfort and security under conditions of peace. Thus, in addition to the virtue of justice we need other traits of character, such as humanity and also what we have called the aspirational virtues that enable us to have or find a sense of purpose in our lives. These other virtues we need both as supports to our being able to sustain the justice virtues and in their own rights as contributory to living well. Humanity, for example, may help us to understand what is just when that is not obvious, when judgement is needed. Humanity may also provide additional motivation for doing what is just when that is difficult. Moreover, humanity enables us to achieve friendship and avoid loneliness – it is a critical component of living well.

If being in business is compatible with living well, it must be possible to do business without having to restrict the concerns that relate to the virtues to one's other non-business activities. Moral virtues, we have argued, are pervasively relevant. If humanity is a moral virtue, it must be just as much part of the framework within which business needs to operate as are honesty and fairness. For a career in business to be compatible with living well, that career needs to be pursued not just as a means to an extraneous end. It must involve activities and practices in which one can take a pride day to day. Since we work out what are moral virtues in relation to our understanding of what constitutes a life worth living, any way of life which, it turns out, requires one to put aside the concerns that are part and parcel of having virtues cannot be compatible with a life worth living.

On the other hand, Elaine Sternberg rightly objects to the notion that we should conduct our business activities by the same standards as we conduct our family lives: 'Different things count as correct conduct for families and businesses, because families and businesses have different functions. Families exist for the mutual care and support of family members, particularly of those, like children and the very old, who are less capable of looking after themselves. A family takes care of its members simply because they are family, without any particular regard for reciprocity or merit; family members are kept and cared for, come what may.'[1] She goes on to say that, 'Business, in contrast, only exists to maximise long-term owner value'.[2] Now, while I do not quite agree with this last – at least, not with the claim that the aim of business is properly to *maximize* as against to *pursue* long-term owner value – I do agree that employees are not owed the same kind of consideration that is owed to members of one's family, and that 'it is not the role of business to give meaning to the lives of its employees'.[3] All the same, employers who are humane will demonstrate this virtue in their business activities, in the way they treat their staff, their suppliers and their customers.

To some extent, their humanity will motivate them to the same practices and policies as does enlightened self-interest. The humane employer may be expected, for example, to discourage 'presenteeism', the tendency of employees to work excessively long hours out of fear for their jobs. So too will enlightened employers who are merely concerned to extract the maximum benefit to the business from their employees. Working longer, is not necessarily working harder or more productively. People's efficiency dwindles and mistakes are made. Moreover, the recent case of Walker v Northumberland County Council (1994) – concerning an over-burdened social worker who suffered a nervous breakdown and then, though his local authority promised relief, suffered a second breakdown when the relief did not materialize – establishes that employers can be held to account for stress-related illness brought on by the excessive demands of work. In the light of such considerations, Elaine Sternberg could argue, without including humanity as of any relevance to the employer's duties, that it is wrong to encourage presenteeism simply because doing so detracts from the maximization of long-term owner value. The humane employer will be concerned to discourage presenteeism, though, whatever the findings of such studies, whether or not these indicate that firms lose more than they gain by allowing or encouraging it.

In this chapter we will explore the responsibilities of employers in respect of two aspects of work: (1) health and safety and (2) hiring, firing and promotion. In each case we will consider how the concerns and requirements relating to virtues bear on what might constitute good (ethically defensible) practice.

Good Practice and a Company's Policy on Health and Safety

On what terms is it ethically defensible to ask employees to do hazardous work? Is it ever defensible? If it is irrational to expose oneself to avoidable risks, then is it not wrong to induce anyone to do that; wrong, then, to pay people to act irrationally? But nobody thinks that taking avoidable risks is *always* irrational. We all do it and we do not censure each other for doing it. Many of us drive about in cars when we do not have to – it is just very convenient. We drive our children to school even though it is safer to walk them there. Parents take their families abroad on holiday, and nobody thinks that they are acting irresponsibly although it would be safer for them to stay at home. It is not necessarily unethical, then, to set up in a business that involves hazardous working conditions.

Given that it is not wrong as such to employ people to do hazardous work, how far are employers responsible for protecting their employees at work, for minimizing the hazards? The law requires employers to 'ensure, so far as is reasonably practicable, the health, safety and welfare at work' of employees.[4] The qualification 'reasonably practicable' allows employers to take into account the *cost* of providing protection. In Hawes v Railway Executive (1952), for example, where the issue was whether it was reasonable to require minor maintenance work to be done near electric rails while the rails were live, it was held that it was not reasonably practicable to switch off the current and disrupt the railway every time it was necessary to do minor maintenance. Of course, the requirement to do all that is reasonably practicable may be interpreted differently by different parties. A business is not required in law to do more than a business of the kind it is can reasonably be expected to do. What that is, is determined *in law* in relation to the prevailing standards and knowledge.

Does morality require more of employers than that they observe whatever legal regulations and guidelines apply in respect of health and safety? How, from a moral standpoint, should employers interpret their obligation to take all reasonable steps to protect employees? Since individuals differ in their evaluation of what risks it is reasonable to take, it might seem that the appropriate way for employers to ensure that their employees are not improperly subjected to risks is both to comply with the legal requirements and besides to make sure that whatever risks employees are subject to at work, they themselves consent to. *Volenti non fit iniuria*: you cannot be wronged if you freely agree to the way you are treated.

This, after all, is the principle that is held to govern good practice in medical experimentation on human subjects. Where people are asked to take part in experiments aimed to benefit others (so-called non-therapeutic research) by putting themselves at risk, the critical moral requirement is generally agreed to be that the volunteers give 'informed consent'. Is this, then, an appropriate principle for employers who aim to be fair and honest with their employees to commit themselves to, where the work to be undertaken is hazardous? Does morality require of employers no less – and no more?

Before we can answer these questions we need to clarify just what counts as 'informed consent'. Understanding what counts is not entirely straightforward, both because of the vagueness surrounding the notion of being informed – you can be more or less informed; information may be more or less relevant; or may be significantly selective; may be more than one person wants to know and less than another wants to know – and because of the equal vagueness of the other requirement for consent to be real, that the consent be *freely* given. Again, we note that freedom admits of degree, and the question arises, how free is free enough for the consent to be real?

Behind the requirement that consent be informed is the idea that if you consent without knowing what it is you are consenting to, your consent is meaningless. Even the law requires that people understand in broad terms what they are consenting to, for their consent to be valid. Doctors seeking consent for certain procedures – for surgery, for example – are required in law to inform patients of certain matters: of risks relating to the procedure recommended, of alternatives and the risks relating to them. From a legal standpoint, they have a duty to get consent that is valid – that the patients understand in broad terms what they are consenting to – *and* they have a duty to inform, so that the patients have explained to them the risks involved in the procedure recommended and also what the alternatives are. Similarly, those who are invited to take part in experimental medical research must give real consent *and* must be fully informed of known risks. But can we extrapolate from the duties of doctors and researchers to define the duties of employers?

How much information do honest and fair employers divulge

regarding the risks their employees are subject to? Honesty should not be confused with openness. Honesty precludes lying, but not, maybe, secretiveness. After all, if honest people cannot keep secrets, they are not to be trusted and it would be highly paradoxical to suppose that being honest is incompatible with being trustworthy. Those who are honest understand just where withholding information does involve a breach of trust. Much will depend on particular circumstances and the kind of context; for example, what is usual practice directly bears on what people can reasonably expect to be told – which is not to say that usual practice is necessarily reasonable.

If you are being interviewed for a job and you are honest, you will not want to lie but you may want to avoid disclosing certain facts that might damage your prospects. Likewise, your interviewer, if honest, will not want to lie to you but might hope to avoid disclosing certain facts that might prejudice you against accepting the job. Your interviewer does not mention to you that the last person who had the job you are applying for was murdered on the premises. The interviewer might reasonably surmise that were you to learn this you might not want the job but not, on that account, see there to be any obligation to inform you. You, for your part, might withhold the information that you have 'done time' for breaking and entering – irrelevant in your view to your suitability for the post to which you are applying since you have long since reformed – but you surmise that your interviewer might not be reasonable about it. Both of you may, of course, be under certain special duties to inform, and in that case, you will, if honest, do so. Duties to inform rely on people not to abuse trust. Honest people do not abuse trust. It might, moreover, be only prudent to inform prospective employees quite fully of any risks involved in a job, before taking them on – but that is another matter.

How free must the employee's consent be for it to count as real? If the work is dangerous, does that not indicate that anyone who agrees to do it, though fully informed, must be desperate? Not necessarily. Someone might be willing to take risks, if the pay is good, even if they could find alternative employment where the pay is adequate. Anyway, even if it is true that your employees only work for you because the alternative for them is dire (unemployment, for example), it does not follow that their consent is not genuine. There is a difference between the lack of freedom to do otherwise that arises from external circumstances and the lack of freedom that may be a factor of how one is prevailed on to do a job. Suppose that you are asked by your doctor to consent to an operation that carries with it serious risks and yet it is pointed out to you that if you do not have the operation you will certainly die. The doctor who tells you this is not forcing you to consent. It is external circumstances that constrict your freedom here and they are not of the doctor's designing. Your consent in the circumstances is still real. Similarly, if your employee reluctantly takes up the job you offer because there is nothing better available, you are not preventing the employee from giving real consent. It would be another matter if you were to ask some of your employees to carry out a particularly dangerous piece of work and to insinuate that those who refuse might be made redundant.

The requirement that employers seek informed consent might seem such as honest and fair employers must applaud. How can it be fair to engage people to do hazardous work, except that they consent and that their consent is genuine – and so they must know what they are consenting to and be free to refuse? As with doctors getting consent for surgery or medical researchers getting volunteers to act a subjects, do not employers too have a duty to inform about the risks involved, where these are not already obvious? Moreover, part of the difficulty in establishing how much protection it is reasonable to provide is that individuals may differ over what trade-offs they regard as reasonable. The principle of informed consent allows the employer to hand over responsibility for deciding how much risk is acceptable to the employees. If they want more protection than is offered they can refuse the work. If enough employees refuse, the employer will 'up' the protection, or perhaps offer danger money as an inducement.

Rather than the employer fixing what level of protection each employee should have beyond the legal minimum, employees might be offered a choice: for example, to don extra protective gear and in consequence work more slowly and make less money or to reject the extra gear so as to be able to work faster and make more money. Compare how individual customers are free to choose what extra safety features they want to pay for when they buy a car over and above those that manufacturers are required to build into all cars.

If employers inform employees of all known risks and make available protective gear and training but allow employees to choose how much attention they pay to their own safety, are they doing all that can reasonably be expected of them from a moral standpoint? Hardly, since many of the risks individuals may choose to take with their own health also carry risks for others – for other employees and for the public at large. Just because an employee is willing to take the risks that attend using drugs, for example, while doing a job, others whom that person puts at risk do not consent. Hence, the reasonableness of a firm such as Toyota in requiring employees to undergo drug screening tests (assuming, that is, that the drug screening tests are reliable and that the drugs being screened for are known to diminish competence).[5] Hence, too, the reasonableness of requiring pilots to undergo frequent health checks and to forfeit their jobs if their fitness becomes questionable.

More problematic is the right to exclude from certain work women who might become pregnant on the grounds that if they do their offspring could be damaged.[6] Though some women might be willing to take that risk, their offspring would not have consented. Is it not reasonable, then, for employers to insist that only those able to demonstrate that they are not at risk of becoming pregnant be allowed such work? Should a firm demand or accept by way of demonstration a formal undertaking by a woman that if she becomes pregnant she will have an abortion? That might seem to depend just on whether abortion is a morally defensible way of dealing with an unwanted pregnancy. If abortion involves murder – as some maintain – then obviously a firm should not encourage it or condone it. But even if it does not involve murder – not, anyway, if carried out very early in pregnancy – there may still be moral objection to a firm demanding or accepting such an undertaking. What if, as could all too easily happen, the woman who has given such an undertaking becomes pregnant and then changes her mind? Abortion is a procedure for which informed consent is required. Neither legally nor morally could she be held to her undertaking.

Suppose that the firm could at modest cost alter the working conditions to eliminate the risk, does it have a moral obligation to do so? If it refuses is it being unfair to women? Not so. A business is not obliged in fairness to make the jobs it offers equally accessible to different categories of candidates provided the basis on which it discriminates is relevant: if a pretty face behind the counter boosts sales, a firm is under no obligation to finance face lifts for the plain faced. Yet, a humane employer might be expected to prefer to eliminate a risk if the cost can be easily absorbed than to sack competent employees. The humane employer would at least look in to this alternative.

We look to the law to impose safety standards generally, both on products and on working conditions. The law can establish a level playing field, making it financially possible for individual firms to conform without thereby being driven out of business by less scrupulous firms. But the law inevitably lags behind new discoveries of hazards. How proactive will the responsible employer be? Again, in some circumstances, being proactive is anyway good business, something to boast about in the market; and if regulations are coming in, it might be economical to begin forthwith to make modifications to fall in line. But suppose that in your particular circumstances being proactive is not advantageous to your pursuit of long-term owner value, are you still morally obliged to be proactive?

If you are honest, you will not abuse the trust of your employees – as, notoriously, Johns-Manville did when it discovered but did not inform its own employees of the hazards of working with asbestos.[7] If a new discovery reveals that your employees' work is dangerous in a way not formerly realized, you have a duty to inform them of this. Similarly, if you as an employee find that you are now in some way posing a risk to your colleagues at work, you have a duty to inform them of this or else you abuse their trust in you. In either case, consent might be renewed to continue work under the altered circumstances. Employees might prefer to run a newly discovered danger or health risk rather than see the firm close down. Colleagues might be willing to take extra precautions rather than see you dismissed. Suppose, though, that there is a health scare that you have good reason to believe to be unscientific: in that case you might know that people would

want you to disclose certain information but you might withhold
it all the same because you do not trust them to behave reasonably. Is it always an abuse of trust to withhold information from
people which they cannot be trusted to treat sensibly?

Let us now return to our question as to whether the moral
obligations of employers in respect of health and safety at work
can be summed up in the requirement to comply with the law
and to secure informed consent from employees. Whatever restrictions the law imposes, there are anyway on all of us constraints on
the use of fraud or force against one another. It is not necessarily
unreasonable to expose employees to risks, but they must know
and consent. Where the risks are not obvious (to employees), they
are owed information. Honest employers not only refrain from
lying, they do not abuse trust either. They will not tolerate a situation where their employees are exposed to risks to which they
would not consent if informed of them.

Getting informed consent is, therefore, necessary, but it is not
sufficient. People may accept risks in order to have a job, yet the
risks could be avoided without excessive cost. The law merely
requires that employers conform to prevailing standards. In some
cultures, and in some kinds of work, people may be apathetic
about injuries, unwilling to demand better protection. A humane
employer will not be content merely to be complying with the
law and to be getting the informed consent of employees. The
humane employer will look for ways of improving safety.

Should the Same Safety Standards Apply in Branches of the Company Abroad?

Is it unjust for a firm to take advantage of the absence of safety
regulations or their effective enforcement in other countries,
employing third-world labourers under conditions that are illegal
back home? It may make a difference to how one should answer
whether the law in these countries does not regulate or whether
it does, but the law is not enforced. There were safety regulations
in India at the time of the Bhopal catastrophe, but in the state in
which Bhopal lies, 'fifteen factory inspectors were given the task
of regulating 8,000 plants; those inspectors, sometimes lacking even

typewriters and telephones, were forced to use public buses and trains to get from factory to factory.'[8] We have supposed that justice, the relevant moral virtue, involves at least conforming to fair laws. Some laws may not be enforced because they are now dead letters. But that is not what we are envisaging here./If the laws imposing safety regulations abroad are just what we should and do insist on at home, they are fair laws, and companies that ignore them simply because they are not enforced are abusing their trust and acting dishonestly.

But suppose that the country in which you choose to locate your branch has few and only minimal safety regulations. These you scrupulously observe. But you have located your branch here just because the absence of safety regulations makes production vastly cheaper than it is back home. Is taking advantage of the predicament of the people you employ in this third-world country ethically indefensible? Is it exploitative?

Taking advantage of people's misfortune's, making money out of them even, is not necessarily exploitative – if, that is, we are understanding 'exploitation' to involve taking _unjust_ advantage. The undertaker who sells a coffin to the family of a murdered man is taking advantage of people's undeserved misfortune – but not necessarily exploiting their misfortune – not if the price is fair and the family has not been tricked into paying more than it would choose if honestly advised. Many jobs are parasitic on other people's misfortunes – doctoring (by and large), social work, insurance agencies – they are not simply on that account, exploitative.

But is the difference of standard you would be tolerating between the conditions you provide to employees back home and the conditions you provide to these third-world employees itself unfair? It need not be. Mere differences of treatment can be justified: they need not involve any unjust attitudes or treatments. It is not unfair, if the third-world employees understand the risks they are incurring and choose to accept them on the terms you offer. It may be rational for them to do so as it would not be for employees back home. Your provision of employment may actually make the situation of the people whom you employ better off than it would be if you did not do so. To be sure, the fact that they tolerate these conditions is an indication of the desperate straits they are in. But that is not of your doing. Your intervention improves their lot as well as yours. In short, the terms of their employment may be such as they can consent to in principle (if informed and wise) – even though those same terms are not such as employees back home could consent to in principle.

There is, though, more to consider than that these employees are being treated fairly. Humane employers will not be satisfied merely that the terms under which they employ people are fair. If the employees are living wretched lives, humane employers will be concerned about this and interested in improving their lot. Humane employers will aim to achieve a profit but not necessarily the maximum possible. Rather, they will pursue a profit that still allows them to act with ordinary decency and with humanity towards their employees. Furthermore, they will take an active interest in encouraging the introduction of regulations to protect safety, not because they confuse their role with that of government but because where they have influence on a government and see an opportunity to promote justice, the protection of basic rights, they will want to use those opportunities. In so acting they may be encouraging social developments that they expect will provide a more stable society and a securer environment for their business involvement in the country, but that will then for them be an additional motive.

To sum up: employers have a moral obligation to conform to fair laws – such as those relating to protection of employees' health and safety. Employers who are honest will not lie to their employees about risks and they will see it as their duty to inform just where failing to inform would involve an abuse of trust – using employees in ways to which they consent only out of ignorance or duress. Humane employers will be on the look out for ways to improve safety at work. Knowing how easily people become lax about safety, even their own safety, and how fastidiousness about safety often has immediate short-term costs (the protective clothing or gear slows up production), employers who are humane will not rely on prevailing social norms and the kind of business they are in to fix the safety standards that are upheld.

On the other hand, humane employers will not disregard costs in considering whether to implement forms of protection over and above what the law requires. The concern of the humane employer to improve safety at work (beyond what the law requires) relates to one kind of ongoing, open-ended, non-dischargeable obligation. The employer's obligation to pursue profits is another such. These obligations can be balanced one against the other. If an employer considers introducing some form of protection beyond what is legally required but decides against on account of the cost, that is not a failure of humanity. Nor, on the other hand, if an employer decides to bear the cost of introducing some form of protection beyond what is legally required, is that automatically a failure of duty to the firm.

Good Practice in Hiring, Firing and Promotion

Everyone appreciates the prudential as well as the moral importance of fair treatment of staff: where fairness is concerned, good business and good ethics may be expected to go hand in hand. Fair treatment (rather, to be precise, the *perception* of fair treatment) is probably the most important factor in motivating employees: 'As the huge corpus of literature on organisational behaviour shows, people are motivated by a great many things but most fundamentally, perhaps, by the desire to be treated fairly'.[9] Of course, the notion is vague; we are all against unfairness, no doubt, but what is fair? What, for example, is fair in respect of hiring, firing and promotion?

Tom Sorell and John Hendry observe that, 'in principle the relations between a business and an employee is governed by a legal contract of employment.'[10] But, as they go on to remark, 'Such contracts often leave out more than they put in'[11] and, in any case, as they note, the moral obligations on both sides may go beyond their legal contracts. Sorell and Hendry proceed to raise questions rather than venture answers as to how employers and employees should work out their reciprocal obligations.

Elaine Sternberg, however, maintains that the principle that should be the basis of ethically defensible business practice is perfectly clear, even if its proper application in some cases can be troublesome. In respect of hiring, firing and promotion the very same constraints apply: selection should be conducted within the law, should be conducted with ordinary decency and in accordance with distributive justice. It should, moreover, subject only to these constraints, be aimed always at the maximization of long-term owner value (by selling goods or services), since that is, she holds, the proper aim of business:

> Fortunately, understanding that business has a defining purpose makes the correct principle of selection [for hiring] very clear: the business should hire that candidate who is expected to contribute most to its purpose of maximising long-term owner value. This principle of selection applies very widely: it indicates who should be hired and who promoted, who should get a rise and (negatively) who should be fired; it even indicates which supplier should be chosen and which procedures should be implemented. Since the principle awards the job or the contract to the candidate whose contribution to maximising long-term owner value is expected to be the greatest, it automatically satisfies distributive justice. In order to be ethical, therefore, selection in accordance with the principle simply needs to be implemented with ordinary decency: honestly, fairly, non-coercively and legally.[12]

This account of the terms under which hiring, firing and promotion are ethically defensible seems to me to be questionable in two respects: (1) in requiring that *the* proper purpose of business is to maximize long-term owner value, and (2) in requiring that selections are unjust if not aimed at selecting the candidate who contributes most (in the case of hiring or promotion) and the one who contributes least (in the case of firing). The second claim follows on naturally enough from the first: if there is an obligation to maximize long-term owner value and if this obligation is an additional constraint on people in business alongside the constraint of ordinary decency. But why must a business be single-mindedly committed to maximizing value? Even if that is one of its avowed commitments, should it not be treated as an ongoing, non-dischargeable, aspirational type of obligation rather than a constraint type of obligation? So regarded, admittedly, the line of duty would not be so clear-cut, as Elaine Sternberg herself points out: 'Only maximizing provides a sufficiently clear-cut, hard-edged criterion of business action.'[13] Part of the appeal of her Ethical Decision Model is its promise to sort out problems over ethically defensible policies and practices. Still, there is no good in having a decision model if it is not reliable.

Elaine Sternberg does allow that people who do business are not morally obliged to pursue what she defines as the aim of business provided that they are self-employed or, if not, that they act with the owners' consent. Furthermore, a corporation, as she points out, need not have as its defining purpose that of doing business: 'Subject only to distributive justice, ordinary decency and local law, the ends sought by the ethical corporation can be anything that the shareholders agree they should be; a corporation need not have a business purpose.'[14] Thus, Elaine Sternberg is defining the term 'business' rather narrowly.[15] She does not object to people defining it more widely to comprehend other sorts of commercial enterprises. The important point on which she insists is that business as she defines it is anyway one kind of activity 'in the modern world' and what is required for it to be conducted in an ethically defensible manner is precisely what her book *Just Business* is about.[16] Plenty of businesses fit her account and it is perfectly reasonable to limit the scope of discussion of business ethics to what constitutes ethically defensible practices and policies just in respect of these.

Elaine Sternberg's fire is directed, then, only at those who are not self-employed, who simply take it upon themselves to divert funds from their business to this or that do-gooding cause when they have no right to do so. What she objects to, in short, is doing good with *other people's money*, vicarious charity – managers who play the Robin Hood. So let us confine our attention to the situation of managers working in the kind of business Elaine Sternberg has in mind. Is she right to insist that they act unethically if they do not aim to maximize long-term owner value subject only to the constraints of distributive justice and ordinary decency?

I suggest this is not plausible, unless one treats the obligation to maximize as readily qualifiable, unless one adds, sotto voce, 'within reason'. Suppose, for example, that you are a manager, that you have worked very hard and successfully all week for your firm, it is a sunny afternoon and you decide to spend it on the golf course: do you have to justify the ethical permissibility of doing so by calculating whether the business will gain more than it loses if you leave your desk? Does any time away from work have to be defended? If the obligation to maximize is not hedged round with the qualification 'within reason', you can never stop work merely because you have done enough, you must always be able to add, 'I can do no more'. If this were so, you would have to justify taking on any other non-business commitments – getting married, for example – with the implausible claim that these commitments would not divert you from the prior commitment to maximize your firm's long-term owner value.

Not only do we recognize that managers are within their rights balancing their working duties with their other commitments, to family and to friends, and with their other interests – taking the day off to go fishing – we also recognize (at least, I suggest that we should) that some actions *at work* can be justified that are diversions from the single-minded pursuit of long-term owner value. The shopkeeper who regularly delivers heavy groceries to elderly customers without charging them, but who charges younger customers, may not be acting in a way that maximizes profits. It is the younger customers who, if any, might shop elsewhere; the elderly are dependent on the shop, so helping them is probably unprofitable. The humane shopkeeper may simply be carrying the elderly customers' groceries to their door because 'it is the decent thing to do' (but it does not fall within Elaine Sternberg's definition of 'ordinary decency'). I submit that the shopkeeper does nothing wrong, at least, if assisting the elderly is not preventing the business from having a reasonable turnover. If you were this shopkeeper you would not owe it to the owners of the business to seek their permission for not charging the elderly – any more than you would to seek their permission before you got married.

Elaine Sternberg maintains that ethically defensible business practice must be in accordance with distributive justice. Distributive justice in respect of hiring, firing or promotion, she claims, involves selecting always whoever is most appropriate, applying the relevant criteria. Given that the aim of business is to maximize long-term owner value, decisions over whom to hire, fire or promote should always be made in accordance with that aim and no other. Injustice in hiring, firing or promoting occurs, then, where individuals are selected on some other basis. Now, if you have *promised* to appoint strictly according to certain criteria, maybe those suggested by Elaine Sternberg, then doing anything else is unjust in that it is a breach of promise. But is it so clear that if you are in the kind of business that is strictly commercial, that you are obliged to single-mindedly maximize profit in all the decisions you take – for example, in hiring, firing or promoting? I suggest that here, too, we should understand the obligation you are under as one that requires maximizing 'within reason', and this allows scope for some other considerations to enter into selection without there necessarily being a breach of contract and without that kind of injustice.

Yet it is often thought that justice requires that the most suitable applicant or candidate be chosen for a position, that whoever is chosen has to be believed to be better, or at least as good as, other candidates, or else one is acting unfairly.[17] Even those who disagree that the best candidate is whichever candidate contributes most to long-term owner value, may at least agree with Sternberg that managers have a duty to appoint whoever is best for the job. But is even this necessarily so? Suppose you have two candidates for one job: Jack and Jill. Both are competent but Jack is more so – more experienced, better references. Yet Jill is good enough. Suppose you choose Jill just because she comes from Edinburgh – as do you. Is this unjust? Who is wronged? Is Jack wronged? Surely not; you have not promised applicants to select the best qualified. You are not obliged to treat candidates like competitors for a prize.[18] Jack has no claim to be chosen. It would be different if you were rejecting him out of prejudice – both illegal and immoral. Are you, though, being unjust to the firm you work for? Why so, if Jill is wholly competent, she will do a satisfactory job – even if Jack might do even better. Of course, it might matter just what the job is, whether it would significantly hurt your firm if you did not select the better candidate – if the job were a sensitive one (the job in question, let us suppose is office cleaning).

Again, suppose that you decide to hire Jill, who is mentally disabled, and who for that reason will need some extra, special training and supervision. Your reason for so doing, let us suppose, is that you have heard how difficult it is for such people to get jobs, how much it means to them and how with help they can perform some jobs quite adequately. Now this particular candidate for the job you have advertised is not best qualified; in fact, she might be, rather obviously, the least qualified – the only applicant with no previous work experience. Is it unjust, then, for you to give her the job? If so, to whom? To the other candidates? But unless you promised (or are legally required) to appoint the best applicant, what wrong are they done? Are you wronging the owners of the business, diverting their money into charity, without their permission? But suppose the cost is small – even if your experiment is a failure. The business may still be able to afford it comfortably. Might you not be justified in trying such a measure, out of mere humanity – though not *obliged* out of humanity to do so? Do you necessarily have to trot off to the owners every time you have an impulse to act humanely, for permission?

All the same, surely Elaine Sternberg is right to castigate employee–managers who distribute largesse that is not theirs to distribute in a cavalier manner to however good causes.[19] My quarrel with her account of ethically defensible business is only that while it is admirably unmoralistic it is also unduly abrasive: I think that manager–employees should understand their obligation to maximize long-term owner value as one that is hedged about with qualifications. To be sure, you may be expected and have agreed 'to do your best' for the firm. But such an undertaking does not have clear-cut obedience conditions: it only makes sense as an aspirational sort of obligation with rather vague conditions attaching to satisfying or more than satisfying what it requires. Compare, the expectation that doctors will do their best for their patients – they are not necessarily failing in their commitment just because they take holidays, or spend extra time at the bedside of patients whom they are fond of – not if in doing so they do not *neglect* the rest of their patients.

Further Reading

On health and safety at work
On legal obligations, see Selwyn, *Laws of Employment*, pp. 209–21 and 410–35; on moral obligations, see Gini, 'Case study – Manville', pp. 89–97, and Coplon, 'When did Johns-Manville know?', pp. 98–100, both discussing the case of Johns-Manville. See also the section on

worker safety in Beauchamp and Bowie, *Ethical Theory and Business*, pp. 189–223, and Braybrooke, *Ethics and the World of Business*, chapter 10, 'Manipulation and exploitation' (mostly about hazardous working conditions).

On hiring, firing and promotion
On unfair dismissal in law, see Selwyn, *Laws of Employment*, pp. 256–342; on moral obligations, see Braybrooke, *Ethics and the World of Business*, chapter 8; Sternberg, *Just Business*, chapter 6; Vallance, *Business Ethics at Work*, chapter 4.

Study Questions

1   If management provides employees with protective gear (for example, safety goggles to its welders) and urges them to wear these, explaining clearly the risks if they do not, is that the limit of its moral obligation in respect of safety protection?

2   Suppose one of your employees, Jack, suffers some visual impairment through an accident unrelated to work, in consequence of which he is now at more risk continuing with his job in the firm. You have fully explained the risks, but Jack wants to carry on even though you offer him another job, less well paid. He suggests that you provide some extra safety equipment which will lessen the risk to him although still not make the job as safe as it was. The extra equipment is quite pricey. If you refuse, are you treating him unjustly? If you refuse to let him carry on, although he accepts the risks, are you treating him unjustly?

3   'All that ethical recruitment does require is that the business hire the candidate likely to contribute most to long-term owner value, and that it observe ordinary decency in its recruitment procedures.'[20]
    How does Sternberg defend this judgement? Do you agree?

10

Good Practice outside the Firm

Good Practice and Treatment of Outsiders

The same moral virtues that underlie good practice among the members of a firm towards each other underlie good practice by members of firms in their dealings with non-members – with suppliers, with customers, with other businesses, with inspectors or with the public at large. But working out just what the virtues involve in particular kinds of contexts – whether, for example, honest business precludes your bluffing in negotiation or your paying accountants to advise on how to minimize your company's tax liability – requires more than sheer common sense and good will. It requires an understanding of the nature of moral virtues in general and of why they matter – understanding which should be helped by ethical theory (by sound theory, that is, – not, for example, by utilitarianism). Theory aside, it also requires understanding of what various practices involve and of the effect that they have on those who are involved in them and on third parties.

Whereas ethical theory in so far as it is sound should apply universally and unchangingly, the nature of particular practices and how these affect people may change. Hence, the same theory applied to a practice in one culture may deem it to be ethically permissible though if applied to the practice in another culture it may not deem it to be so – because 'the practice' is significantly different. Thus, for example, it could be that some types of deception by doctors of their patients, which used to be commonplace, expected and, for the most part, condoned by both parties, were not dishonest *then* though they would be if attempted by our doctors nowadays. Honesty would have been no less important between doctors and patients then than now, but what being honest involved would not have been quite the same.

Compare how Jews nowadays who stand by the traditional Jewish prohibition on usury if practised by Jews on Jews – on lending money at interest – might still view differently from their forebears the acceptability of bank loans – deemed to fall within the prohibition once, now perhaps not to. Arguably, the nature of lending has changed significantly: 'Business loans today, as distinct from the moneylending which characterized banking until the 19th century, are, in effect, investments rather than simple loans against collateral.'[1] As we noted earlier (chapter 2), our map of morality may need revising from time to time – and not always because the former map was inferior but because the lie of the land has changed somewhat.

In the previous chapter we explored the responsibilities of employers towards their own employees in respect of health and safety, and, in respect of hiring, firing and promotion, their responsibilities to their own actual or would-be employees. In this chapter let us reflect on the responsibilities that members of firms have towards those outside the firm with whom they deal or who are affected by their dealings. We will confine our discussion to two areas:

1   *Just dealing*: whether any practice that is deliberately deceptive or furtive is automatically ruled out – spurned by those who are honest.
2   *Green business*: to what extent a business is obliged to contribute to or support environmental concerns beyond those obligations that are legally imposed.

Just Dealing

Let us understand 'just dealing' to refer to dealings that are not unjust. By 'just dealing' we do not here mean dealing that accords with the law of the land, but dealing that accords with what we have called the regulatory rules of morality – the rules that any society needs to recognize and uphold if it is to maintain the peace. We have already defined wrongdoing as doings that violate these rules, and we have noted that these rules basically impose constraints on our use of force and fraud as ways of achieving our aims – whatever these are, whether worthy or otherwise.

These rules, obviously, are not exceptionless. The general presumption is against our resorting to force or fraud to achieve our aims, but we acknowledge that some uses are necessary and some permissible. The necessary exceptions will relate to types of use that are actually necessary *for* our living in peace: we need law enforcement, for example, and effective law enforcement may require that police be permitted to use force or fraud to achieve that aim (we see the necessity of police on occasion carrying arms, or on occasion wearing plain clothes).

The permissible exceptions will relate to types of uses that do not undermine the peace. What these latter types of exceptions will have in common, I suggest, is that they do not involve abuse of trust or of a position of trust. That is why they do not threaten the peace. Thus, for example, our living in peace does not require that we should repudiate all types of lying, whatever the context. But our tolerance of some types of lies needs strict containment to agreed exceptions – to contexts where the lying does not abuse trust. What these contexts are may need to be sorted out differently in different societies and in different circles within a society.

Honesty and Just Dealing

The law of the land does not oblige you to refrain from lying generally. Lying in court is perjury; lying in your own office, to your colleague, is not a criminal offence. But I have claimed that honesty is a virtue, one of the justice-virtues, so to speak. If this is correct, honesty must be something that matters for all of us in all of our dealings, whether we are in business or not and whether the dealings we are engaged in are with members of our own firm or with outsiders. It is obvious enough that a reputation for dishonesty does a business no good at all. Moralists will claim that it is crazy to risk a bad reputation and that the only safe way to avoid that is actually to be honest. Still, it is undetected dishonesty that might pay off – for all that moralists claim. And just how often people get away with *that* is, as R.E. Ewin observes, in the nature of the case, hard to assess.[2]

Anyway, I have argued that honesty is quite squarely located in the justice family of virtues and that these virtues are essential components of lives worth living. Moreover, even if some people manage to prosper in business who are not honest, I have claimed (see chapter 6) that it is quite possible for people who are honest to prosper in business too. In short, my claim is that while you might be successful in business though you are not honest, you cannot be successful in business *and* in life unless you are honest. By 'successful in life' I mean making the most of the chances life offers you to have a life worth living (see chapter 5).

But can it really be that honesty is so essential to living in peace – seeing, as we know very well, that people are often dishonest and so it has always been? Surely society can weather a good deal of dishonesty – can, because it does. Similarly, we cannot say that society presupposes that people abjure violence against one another since violence is commonplace and always has been. There is a difference, though, between a society repudiating force and fraud in principle and its managing to keep in step in practice. Commitment to the principle is more important than success in keeping in step – provided the commitment is sincere. We expect people to lie and to commit assaults. We struggle to keep such behaviour within bounds – because we appreciate that life would become intolerable if we gave up altogether. The fact that we anticipate assaults and lies does not indicate that we are complacent about their occurrence. We can know that we will tell lies – inexcusably: because we are only human and past record makes future lapses all too predictable. All the same, we may not *intend* to tell (inexcusable) lies. Society may get by despite our many actual lapses provided, though, that we do not become so used to lying and being lied to that we become indifferent about it.

We have already noted (in chapter 6) that the cost of being honest in business can easily be exaggerated. Honesty should not be confused with candour (openness). A person can be both secretive and honest. To be trustworthy one needs to be both. Candour is not a virtue just because candour is not always morally appropriate. Candour to the media about the personal habits of one's employer may be a betrayal of trust. The honest employee understands when there is a duty to inform, when it is permissible to inform and when it is not. Candour is owed to some and not to others, about some matters, not about others. Hence, furtiveness is not always dishonest.

Moreover, I maintain, that you can be honest and be deliberately deceptive. Deliberate deception is not necessarily dishonest. Deliberate deception is not dishonest, I have suggested, just where it does not involve an abuse of trust.[3] There are different kinds of ways in which a lie, for example, might not, in the circumstances involve an abuse of trust. You might, for example, find yourself in a dilemma: you are being questioned in court about a matter that you are bound to keep secret. The surest way of preserving the secret might be to tell a downright lie. Of course, the law directs you out of the dilemma: you must never commit perjury. But that is not necessarily how morality directs you. Lying in court is never trivial. All the same, the confidence that you are trying to preserve may be such as to justify even perjury. If it does then your lying, in the circumstance, is not an abuse of trust. Another possibility is that although the matter you are being pressed to reveal is not confidential, revealing it would cause great harm. Here, again, you might decide correctly that to avert this harm the lie is justified – and is not in the circumstances an abuse of trust.

The above kinds of 'dilemma' relate to situations where a lie that would otherwise be wrong, might not on the occasion in question be so. But I maintain that there are also *types* of deception that do not involve abuse of trust, types that honest people may engage in. Deception in negotiation may be a case in point.

Deception in Negotiation

Consider the common practice of lying about one's reservation price when negotiating a deal. To be sure, the mere fact that lots of people do it and suffer no qualms of conscience about it does not show that it is ethically defensible – only that they think it is.

Some people will say that 'sending out misleading messages' is simply part of the 'art of bargaining';[4] some will say that it is a necessary tactic in a morally flawed world – morally regrettable but justified where you are dealing with people who cannot be trusted.[5] In either case, though, you are operating in what may be called a 'trust-deficient social context'[6] – that is, you lie about your reservation price in the expectation that those with whom you are dealing will lie about theirs. Supposing that this assumption is reasonable on your part – you are familiar with the conventions observed by the people with whom you are dealing – if you do not follow the customary negotiating strategy, you will not inspire trust but contempt and mistrust: you are not playing the game you are supposed to play. Far from your lying tactic undermining trust, you are more likely to do that by bargaining and not lying.

But would honest people not, then, at least refuse to bargain in such circumstances? Is the only honest course where you realize that those with whom you would deal expect to haggle, to withdraw? Will honest people at least consider this a regrettable practice, which they would like to see the end of? Why so? Why should they object to this any more than they object to games of bluff, or to the routine deceptions practised in sport: tennis players who pretend to be aiming the ball in a particular direction are not tainted with dishonesty or lack of commitment to the concerns of justice? Alan Strudler contends that where the convention of deception in bargaining is understood, this type of deception actually has 'strong moral credentials': 'a fair and mutually advantageous practice that allows people to negotiate, while limiting the risks they face'.[7] Be that as it may, at least, it seems, that this type of deception does not involve an abuse of trust and need not in any way undermine trust. I suggest, therefore, that business people who go in for it are not being dishonest, and quite possibly honest business people will see no objection to it.

It might be argued, though, that haggling does not necessarily involve lying at all – not if lying involves saying what is false with the intention to deceive. Where haggling is the convention, you do not expect those with whom you bargain to believe you when you announce what your reserve price is. Is this an instance of the *conventional* lie which is *not* actually a lie – any more than artificial silk is silk? Compare how routinely we tell 'little' lies out of

politeness or to avoid embarrassment or to spring a pleasant surprise: pretending, for example, to be interested in what someone
is telling you, pretending to be surprised by the present your children have attempted to keep secret, pretending to believe someone's
excuse for not visiting you although you do not believe it.

Maybe, though, with all these conventional lies, the aim is indeed
to deceive, even if the aim is sometimes rather half-hearted. Listening to the tedious story and pretending interest, you prefer *not*
to be noticed peeping at your watch. Haggling with experienced
hagglers you do not take at face value the opening bids, but you
treat them all the same as indicators of the range within which the
negotiation will proceed. What is said gives some information but
of limited reliability. Each side has a chance of getting the better
of the other, because the other may be finally, successfully deceived
about the actual reservation price. Similarly, in a game of tennis,
just because the players are *expecting* misleading signals from each
other does not stop them successfully sending those signals.
Knowing that someone is trying to deceive you does not entirely
arm you against their doing so.

It might be thought that the reason why bluffing in negotiation is not dishonest – even if you *are* telling outright lies – is just
that those with whom you are dealing do not have the usual *right*
to not be lied to: those who themselves tell lies or otherwise violate the regulatory rules of morality forfeit the right to be treated
according to those rules. This might be thought a clearer way of
identifying those types of deception that are defensible, of which
honest people could approve, than the common feature I elicit,
that the defensible deceptions do not 'abuse trust'.

We can agree that those who tell lies have no right not to be lied
to – how can their trust be *abused*? They have no right to trust
others if they are themselves untrustworthy. But we should not
agree that what makes lying wrong (when it is wrong) is *just* that
the person lied to is being wronged. If it *were* permissible to lie
to those who tell lies, we would seldom need to be honest. The
duty we are generally under not to lie holds even where those
with whom we are dealing are evidently not honest. We owe it,
not to the other party, but to society: because commitment to
honesty is socially necessary. Thus, though it will be true that the
types of lies that are defensible will be such that the persons lied to

have no right in the circumstances not to be lied to, since defensible lying involves no abuse of trust, it does not follow that wherever individuals forfeit the right you are justified in lying to them.

Tax Evasion and Exploiting Legal Loopholes

Another common practice in business is to employ accountants to advise on how to minimize tax liability. Is this something that honest business people will disdain or, on the contrary, is it not only ethically permissible to seek to minimize tax liability, but irresponsible *not* to do so? Doubtless, Elaine Sternberg would argue that if you are managing a commercial firm you owe it to the shareholders to maximize long-term owner value and therefore you should not be paying any tax beyond what is legally required. Paying experts to advise on legal ways of cutting down on the tax you pay will be sound business strategy and ethically respectable.

Would she not be dead right? There is no abuse of trust in a business paying no more than is legally required. If there are legal loopholes overlooked by legislators, it is their job to remove them. It is not as if there is a prior moral obligation to pay taxes, which the legal requirement is underwriting: the obligation is created, not acknowledged, by the law.[8] Nor need honest business people feel any obligation to call attention to the loopholes their accountants find for them. Their furtiveness in the matter is innocent. There is nothing fraudulent, dishonest or ethically remiss about their trying to keep secret the ways they find to evade taxes, provided, of course, these ways are legal. A recent newspaper headline reads: 'MPs save thousands through tax loopholes' – a report which can be expected to embarrass, but should not shame, those named.[9]

Contrast how a company might spot a loophole in the law that would enable it legally to discharge toxic waste. Now, this surely raises quite different considerations. The law that is failing to do its job here is one that is intended directly to protect people's lives and health – you may know that although the discharge is not illegal, it is liable to cause serious illness to many people. In this case, the mere fact that it is not illegal does not mean that you need not give the matter a second thought.[10] It is one thing to hire an accountant to advise you on how to minimize your tax liability, quite another to hire a legal expert to advise on how to legally circumvent new safety legislation. Even so, if there is a known loophole that your business rivals are all exploiting, you may be forced to do so too if you are to stay in business. Only legislation can restore a level playing field.[11] Those in the business who are concerned that people are being exposed to such dangers may be expected to campaign for better legislation. There is no excuse for furtiveness in this kind of case.

Green Business: Obligations of Business in Respect of the Environment

Do businesses have obligations beyond whatever may happen to be required by law, to follow policies and practices that protect the environment for future generations of humans? Our account of obligations and virtues – what they are and why they matter – derives from considerations of the kinds of constraints and commitments our living satisfactorily as human beings requires of us. Satisfactory living requires that we acquire certain virtues of character that enable us to trust and be trusted, that enable us to deal justly with one another. But isn't the idea of dealing justly with distant future generations of humans a nonsense? What kind of contract can there be between us and posterity – what could posterity do for us in return for what we might do for them? How can posterity have rights when posterity does not even exist? From actual (existing) rights, it may be said, spring actual (existing) obligations; from hypothetical (non-existing) rights, spring merely hypothetical (non-existing) obligations.

Yet while rights would seem to imply corresponding duties, duties do not necessarily imply corresponding rights. I may have incurred a duty to look after your cacti – because I have promised to do so. It does not follow that the cacti have rights to my care. Cacti are not plausible bearers of rights – they cannot explain their rights, waive them, abuse them, forget them or demand them. Still, one may have an obligation or duty to one party to bestow benefit on a third party, the latter not being a party to the contract.

Couples when they marry may make pledges to one another to share in parental responsibilities – for example, to bring up their children in accordance with a particular faith. Such pledges are equally intelligible whether or not the offspring in question is already on the way.

Accordingly, it is possible that we have duties in respect of future generations, to make provision for them, even though they do not yet exist. But, if so, whence does this kind of obligation arise? To whom might we owe such an obligation, given that we cannot owe it directly to posterity? Might it be that we owe a debt of gratitude to our forebears, who made sacrifices for our benefit in the expectation that we in turn would do our bit for posterity? Even supposing it is true that many of our predecessors thought of themselves as stewards of the world's resources and sought to leave the world for their successors as good or better than they found it, chances are, they were concerned particularly for their own progeny. If they were not putting themselves out to benefit us, even if because of what they did we stand to benefit, gratitude as opposed to thankfulness seems out of place. Suppose, though, that we have reason to think that they acted as public benefactors – endowing scholarships, hospitals, libraries for the benefit of posterity – so that we are genuinely in their debt, how can we repay such a debt to them since they no longer exist? Debts of gratitude can surely only be paid by doing good to those to whom they are owed. How can you do good to people now dead?

Perhaps, after all, you can. We should not just assume that only the living have interests – that it is not possible to harm or benefit the dead. Aristotle comments on the saying, 'Call no man happy before he is dead'. Actually even death does not necessarily seal one's fate for better or for worse. It would be a great misfortune to have one's property wrecked, one's children murdered, one's reputation blighted *after* one's death even if it would be even more unfortunate to suffer such events while still alive. We do, after all, care about what happens after our lives as well as during them. It matters to us that our friends, our children, the causes we espouse should continue to prosper. Thus, if the debt of gratitude is paid by doing good to those to whom you owe it, their death need not be an obstacle. You can do the dead good by fulfilling their wishes

– or harm by acting against their wishes. If they made sacrifices for us, they must have thought it reasonable to do so. It is likely that they would have hoped that we would be similarly inclined, that they would have wished us to do our bit for posterity just as they did for us.

This argument rests on premises that are not obviously true and are difficult to establish: did our forebears put themselves out in order to preserve the world or to make it better for us? If not, we owe them nothing. Even if we suppose that they did, we might acquit ourselves by benefiting posterity in other ways than by preserving the environment. However, if the conservationists' warnings about the extent to which the global environment is threatened are well-founded, there would be a strong case for giving environmental concerns first priority.

There is, perhaps, another route by which to establish that we, if we are *able* to act effectively to protect the environment for future generations, have an obligation to do so. Consider the duties we have in respect of our friends, to care for their well-being now and in the future. Those we love – friends, family – we want to prosper. We want them to continue to prosper after we are dead and gone. The fortunes of those we love are inextricably bound up with our own, and just as we take thought for our own personal future well-being, so do we also on behalf of our friends.

Now, by the same token, our friends will have reason to act to protect the well-being of their (other) friends whose fortunes are inextricably bound up with their own. And do we not then, also have reason to act to safeguard the fortunes of our friends' friends? Moreover, is it not to be expected that we and our friends have some friends who belong to the next generation, for example, our own, or their, children? They in turn will have some friends of the succeeding generation – and so on. Thus, just as we have a reason to safeguard the fortunes of our friends, we have also a reason to safeguard the fortunes of some members of succeeding generations, including those who would suffer were a calamity of the kind forecast by the conservationists to befall posterity. To be sure, there are obvious practical considerations that justify our paying more attention to safeguarding the well-being of our own friends than that of our friends' friends. But if it were clearly established by the conservationists that unless we who are able to act now do so, calamity will certainly befall posterity, would we not owe it out of friendship to act? We do not need fine details about the tastes and preferences of posterity to appreciate that they at least will need air fit to breathe and water fit to drink.

But how credible is this attempt to derive a duty to posterity from our duty to our existing friends? Is it true that we have reason to care for the fortunes of friends of our friends? If Mary loves John and John loves Joan it does not follow that Mary has reason to love Joan. It is not irrational for Mary to hate Joan just for the very reason that John loves her. We love our children. We do not necessarily have a reason to love their friends and to wish them well. There are friends and friends. People are not always fortunate in their choice of friends or in their ability to distinguish true friends from false. Prudence, then, requires that we seek out and recognize our true friends – it is only *their* fortunes that are inextricably bound up with our own. The duty to posterity can still be derived from the duty of friendship, then, provided we understand the latter duty to hold only in respect of our true friends. The lines of true friendship descend down through succeeding generations to posterity. Hence, in so far as the fortunes of posterity depend on what we do now, we have reason to act to safeguard their fortunes.

This argument assumes the unimportance of *distance* over time: our reason to act now to avert calamity later is not undermined by the fact that those who would be affected do not yet exist and will not for some time to come. Is this assumption reasonable? To test it, let us consider the following scenario. Let us suppose that you are a young woman about to marry and intending to have children. You and your intended seek genetic counselling and discover that you have a rare condition that is genetically transferable to your children, which would cause them to go blind in later life but which you can avoid transmitting to your offspring if only you abstain from eating chocolates (to which you are partial) for several months before you conceive. Granted that your fortune is inextricably bound up with those of the children you intend to have – for you reasonably expect your children to be true friends to you – you have a reason to abstain from chocolates during the critical period. It neither signifies that the children whose fortunes you are making sacrifices for do not yet exist nor that the calamity they would otherwise suffer would probably not befall them in your own lifetime.

Suppose the genetic defect, you are told, will skip a generation – or skip several. Do you have any less reason to abstain then? Only, surely, if you have reason to believe that in the interim some way will be found to correct the genetic defect. The mere fact that the calamity would occur later rather than sooner is not otherwise a reason for you to treat it more lightly. Thus if the conservationists can show that calamity is sure to befall posterity unless we act now – that there is no chance of future technology coming to the rescue – we should simply discount as irrelevant the fact that the calamity is not forecast to happen in the near future.

Admittedly, we probably do not feel that the fate of our great great grandchildren is as important to us as is that of our own children. But we know that our feelings are not always reliable touchstones of what matters to us. Typically, we feel less concerned about doing well in our exams when these are months away than when they are weeks or days away – yet the importance to us of doing well in them is hardly likely to be affected correspondingly. That we generally give more thought to the fortunes of our children than to those of our great great grandchildren is of course only rational since we are generally in a better position to affect the fortunes of the former than the latter for better or worse.

What we have reason to do and what we have a duty to do does, though, depend on what is possible and at what cost. Much as we may wish to protect posterity, we may realize that individually our efforts will not signify. Only if we are in a position to act collectively in a manner that stands fair chance of being effective have we an obligation. It is hardly likely that individual firms who adopt environmentally-friendly policies and practices will have a significant effect on the prospects of posterity. Some might be able to use their influence to encourage and support collective action that would be effective and significant. For some firms, though, unilateral commitment to environmental policies and constraints, beyond those imposed by law, would be both costly and ineffective. Thus, even if we are agreed that we have an obligation to protect prosperity and that this requires the general cooperation of businesses in environmentally-friendly practices and policies, it does not follow that a particular business which is only as environmentally-friendly as the law requires of it is acting unethically. Whether the duty to posterity derives from our duty of gratitude to our forebears or from our duty to our friends, it is in either case an open-ended aspirational type of duty. A firm is not necessarily remiss if it reckons that there is nothing it can sensibly do on the environmental front beyond complying with the law.

All the same, a firm that was on the look-out for loopholes in environmental regulations to exploit, as a way of stealing a march on its competitors, would be remiss – at least if the pollution it was causing was believed to threaten human health. We have noted that a firm's moral obligation to protect health and safety is not just created by the law. The same holds for pollution, even that which only harms the health of future generations, if, as I have argued, we have obligations in respect of future generations. It is one thing for a firm to pass up, because of the cost, an opportunity to reduce its contribution even more than it is required by law to do; it is another for a firm to seize an opportunity to evade an environmental regulation on discovering a legal way of doing so.

But suppose you are chief executive in a commercial firm and you apply the principles for ethically defensible business practice spelled out by Elaine Sternberg: act within the law; observe distributive justice and ordinary decency, with the aim in all your actions, subject only to these constraints, to maximize long-term owner value.[12] Would you not then be remiss in *not* seizing opportunities, even seeking them out, of getting round environmental or any other regulations in ways that are legal? Ordinary decency, as defined by Sternberg, debars you from dishonesty, unfairness, use of coercion or physical violence. It does not require anything more, and the maximizing duty would seem to rule out any other constraint as positively unethical. Surely, though, evasion of regulations is not all on a par, regardless of the kind of regulations in question. Whereas I agree with the Sternberg principles applied in respect of legal evasion of taxes, I suggest that evasion with respect to human health and safety, hence some aspects of environmental regulation, is not morally on a par – though, if only the Sternberg principles apply, it should be.

Further Reading

On honesty
See Sissela Bok, *Lying*.

On honesty in marketing
See Carr, 'Is business bluffing ethical?'; Jackson, 'Honesty in marketing'.

On deception in negotiation
See Sissela Bok, *Lying*, chapter 9; Strudler, 'On the ethics of deception';
  Dees and Cramton, 'Deception and mutual trust'.

On obligations to future generations
See Barry and Sikora, *Obligations to Future Generations*; Partridge,
  Responsibilities to Future Generations; Attfield, *The Ethics of Environmental
  Concern*.

Study Questions

1   'If the truth hurts, tell a lie. This is the advice from the Life Insur-
    ance Association (LIA), the group that claims to represent the pro-
    fessional adviser,' writes Naomi Caine.[13]
        When, if ever, do you think that telling a lie to avoid hurt (to
    whom?) is ethically justified? Might it sometimes be defensible to
    deliberately deceive, but not with an outright lie? If so, why?
2   'I worked in the office of a company that distributed spare parts
    for heavy machinery throughout northern Michigan. When
    somebody would call in for a part, we would look up the number,
    price and inventory level on the computer. The boss told us
    always to say that we had the part in stock, even if the inventory
    level showed us that we were out, that we didn't have any left.
    His argument was that we could always get the part from Chicago
    in a day or two and that a day or two was not going to hurt
    anyone. I didn't like it because it meant I had to lie to somebody
    about once a day.'[14]
        Is this, in your view, an example of defensible lying? Justify
    your view. Is your answer here consistent with your answer
    regarding this same scenario in study question 3(i) in chapter 7?

3 Some retailers, struggling to survive a downturn in sales, will take advantage of loopholes in the Department of Trade's code of practice in order to mislead customers into thinking they are being offered a bargain. 'One of the most frequent abuses involves displaying a sales price against a recommended retail price (RPP). This is allowed as long as the RPP is provided by a manufacturer or supplier "as a price at which the product might be sold to consumers". In some cases, however, manufacturers are in league with retailers to provide them with an inflated price so that they can make it appear they are offering a big reduction.'[15]

Is this an ethically defensible sales strategy so long as the loophole in the code of practice remains? Would it meet the criteria laid down by Elaine Sternberg for ethically defensible commercial practice?

4 'We almost all agree that equal respect for people as human beings is in some sense imperative, but when it gets down to most particular cases it is not at all clear what it is supposed to mean.'[16]

Do you agree that just dealing requires 'equal respect'? What sense do you attach to the notion of 'equal respect'? Are future generations owed equal respect with the present generation?

5 Does a commercial business have any moral obligation to protect the environment other than by conforming to the law? Justify your answer.

11

Virtues, the Key to Good Practice

Why Virtues?

An account of morality that takes as its starting point moral virtues scores over both rights- or duty-based and utility-based accounts, at least in its ability to make sense of the *importance* of morality – and so, of good practice. Utilitarians simply posit their starting point, the moral necessity of maximizing everyone's happiness or satisfaction of preferences or welfare. Those who adopt rights-based accounts also posit their starting point – in this case, some general right declared to be basic, such as, for example, that everyone is owed equal concern and respect. In neither case, does the theory *explain* why it is important for you or me to follow good practice if that is what following it involves. These theories are demanding without being motivating.

Compare how, if good practice is a matter of having virtues and acting accordingly, the importance of good practice is undeniable. We all have reason to support good practice since we all want our lives to go well – our *own* lives; but this is not necessarily a selfish want – typically, we see our own lives as going well only if the lives of our children, our close friends, our parents, go well. The moral virtues, as here defined, are just those traits of character we need in order to have the best chance of making our lives go well. Since these virtues relate to fundamental universal facts about human nature and conditions of living tolerably, they are of critical importance for all people everywhere.

Thus, for example, all people are subject to the raw emotion of anger; can learn to control it; are advantaged to the extent that they develop judgement in how they channel it and are blamed if they fail to develop judicious control over it. Having this control and judgement is, moreover, pervasively relevant and advantageous to us – in friendship, at work, when at play; whether we are leading or being led, whether we belong to primitive or to highly sophisticated societies. Similarly, there are certain conditions of life that apply to all people everywhere, such as our need to elicit cooperation and tolerance from one another. To a significant extent, our success in coping with this need depends on our developing certain social traits of character, which are virtues – for example, humanity and justice.

Justice versus Utility

A virtues-based theory not only makes better sense of the importance *of* morality, it also makes better sense of the importance *in* morality of justice considerations in relation to considerations of utility. Consider, on the one hand, the familiar objection to utilitarian theory that it fails to explain adequately the importance in morality of justice-type considerations – individual rights seem too easily swamped by whatever makes for maximum satisfaction overall, for example, for the public at large. Consider, on the other hand, the familiar objection to duty- or rights-based theories that these fail to accommodate adequately the importance in morality of utility considerations – whether there is a duty to do good and if there is, how conflicts between it and other duties are to be resolved.

A virtues-based approach scores over these theories in that it explains how those who have virtues are bound by certain constraint-type obligations but also to pursue other, aspirational-type obligations. Both types of obligation influence how those who have the virtues conduct themselves – as we have seen in our study of the attitude of employers who are humane and just, towards issues of health and safety at work (see chapter 9).

For a further demonstration of the superiority of the virtues-based approach we have adopted, consider how it may be applied to help resolve some of the problems that are said to be of primary ethical concern in regard to international business. Manuel Velasquez suggests that neither utilitarian nor contractarian (rights-based) approaches to business ethics resolve satisfactorily some of the most pressing ethical concerns in the field.[1] These most pressing problems, he argues, have to do with the ease with which businesses based in rich countries can take advantage of the relative lack of might of poor countries to amass huge profits for themselves, while the poor countries on which they prey benefit very little.

He instances the way in which aluminium companies obtained their ore from Jamaica in the 1960s and 1970s, making enormous profits for themselves while Jamaica was able to take very little advantage of having under its own soil the basic resources out of which these profits ultimately flowed. Velasquez points up the business strategies that enable companies to get away with such conduct. These include: minimal capital investment, for example, not sharing any of the technology with the host countries – in the case of Jamaica, most of the companies only mined the ore from the ground in Jamaica and then shipped the bauxite to their home country for further, more profitable processing; transfer price manipulation – so as to evade local taxes; monopoly control of the world market – as soon as Jamaica tried to gain more control, for example, by imposing levies, the foreign companies transferred their operations elsewhere and Jamaica was unable to compete against them; payment of wages to local employees that are barely above subsistence level.

Velasquez argues that, although the injustice of such conduct is clear, neither a utilitarian nor a rights-based theory can explain why it is wrong. In fact, from a utilitarian standpoint, to establish whether such conduct *is* wrong we need to work out whether, all things considered, the consequences of such conduct fail to maximize utility: 'But how are we to know which actions of the aluminium companies would have maximised utility?' Velasquez asks.[2] As he says, 'there is no way of answering that question because the information requirements that doing so would place on us are simply insurmountable'.[3] And even if the misery of Jamaicans *were* outweighed by the happinesses of all those who profited from the actions of these companies, would it not in any case have been unjust to deny Jamaicans a significant share of the profits?

Velasquez maintains that a rights-based approach is also inadequate when applied to this type of conduct, since it is quite possible that the companies who act in these ways do not violate any basic human rights. He considers, by way of example, the ten basic rights laid down by Thomas Donaldson[4] (allegedly derivable from a social contract, though Velasquez notes that Donaldson does not endeavour to show how). Donaldson maintains that while a business must not violate these rights nor act in ways that undermine them, it is not under a positive duty to secure these rights in the countries in which it operates. From this standpoint, then, the companies that go in for this sort of conduct do nothing wrong and do not deserve censure.

Consider, now, what we should say, applying our virtues-based approach, of this type of conduct. Those who are just will comply with fair laws and regulations. They will not, therefore, engage in strategies that are in fact illegal or that they have bound themselves not to participate in. But suppose that the strategies at issue are not illegal – though clearly hurtful to poor countries like Jamaica. A practice may, of course, be unjust though not illegal. Slavery, to take an obvious example, was always unjust but has not always been illegal. Velasquez regards the conduct he describes as inherently unjust – because while both the parties to these transactions benefit thereby, the benefits fall so (inordinately) heavily in favour of the powerful: 'The real ethical issue is the meagre contribution they made relative to the enormous revenues they collected.'[5] It is the pronounced *inequality* of benefit that Velasquez seems to identify as unjust. But is it?

Suppose that the transaction were between a very rich country and a fairly rich country, would it still seem unjust? If transactions are only just if both parties benefit pretty equally, few transactions will be just. A transaction is not unjust provided it (1) is legal, (2) is freely and informedly consented to and (3) does not violate anyone's moral rights. We surely do not have to add: (4) both parties to the transaction are equally pleased with the terms.

Surely, if there is injustice in conduct of the kind Velasquez criticizes it is not because of the *inequality* of benefits accruing to each party, but rather because one of the parties is in desperate straits and there is a duty to help those in such acute need. But is this a duty of justice or a duty of humanity? Either way, it is a duty of the aspirational, open-ended type. We have noted that those who are just – who have the relevant virtue, or set of virtues – have two distinct kinds of concern: a primary concern not them-selves to act unjustly and a secondary concern to promote justice in the world. Whereas contractarians, as Velasquez points out, con-fine moral duty to the former concern, the largely 'negative' duty, to avoid acting unjustly oneself, the virtues approach recognizes that there is the other kind of 'positive' duty, the duty to promote justice – for example, to prevent others from acting unjustly. This latter duty is no less binding than the former constraint-type duty but it binds in a *different* way.

Business people who are humane and just will not themselves act inhumanely or unjustly. Nor will they be indifferent to inhu-manity or injustice done by others. But that is not to say that if they truly care they will take every opportunity that comes their way to act in the cause of justice or humanity. Still, we should expect them generally to show interest in opportunities to fur-ther these causes – for example, that if they were involved in international business, they would be supporting (and enthusi-astically, not grudgingly) the introduction of codes like the Organ-ization for Economic Cooperation and Development (OECD) Guidelines for Multinational Enterprises (1976). Such measures have the advantage of establishing a level playing field so that the limitations on what rich countries can make out of poor ones are shared.

In short, transactions do not have to benefit all concerned equally in order to be just. The deal that a business makes with employees abroad may be conspicuously less equal than what it could make back home. That of itself is not proof that the deal abroad is unjust or inhumane. All the same, people in business who are themselves just and humane will not simply ignore inhumanity or injustice, which their employees abroad suffer from. A recent *World in Action* programme has claimed that Marks & Spencer sells clothes made in Morocco by children – children under 15.[6] It is not in fact illegal in Morocco for children over 12 to work. But Marks & Spencer vigorously repudiates the use of children under 15 as totally abhorrent.[7]

That may be wise policy in terms of public relations with UK consumers. But given the predicament of the Moroccan children who seek work, is it morally unjust to employ them? Are their rights better protected or respected if they are refused work? Perhaps what should surprise us in these allegations against a company that has always adopted a high moral tone about how it does business, is not that it may be making use of child labour but that the young workers filmed, whether they are 14 or 16, do not seem to benefit in any way from working for a prosperous foreign company which is committed to ensuring that all who provide its wares understand and support its high standards of 'good human relations at work'.[8] One might expect that as a matter of course Marks & Spencer would be including among the good causes it promotes some initiative relating to the working conditions or welfare of these lowly suppliers of wares.

Yet, introducing initiatives that are not mere gestures, that are genuinely beneficial to the recipients when these belong to a very different culture from one's own may not be so easy as onlookers assume. Absence of initiative is no proof of lack of concern. And, of course, we are not entitled to assume that there have been no such initiatives, merely because none surfaced in this particular television programme. Such trial by television 'exposures' are often protested against by those targeted. A report, even if factually accurate, may still be unfair and misleading. Those who are criticized will, doubtless, say that unless one understands the context in which decisions are made and acted on, one is not competent to pass judgement.

The Relevance of Virtues

Indeed, the whole project of this book may be challenged along these lines. How can philosophical ethics be a suitable source of guidance to people in business? Is it not hopelessly out of touch with the realities of business life? How can it be relevant? The very idea that people in business will be interested in opportunities to promote just or humane causes (except, of course, as mere publicity stunts) may sound laughable. If everyone were honest, one might want to be honest too. But given that others are opportunistically dishonest, isn't it only rational to 'go with the flow'?

The world of commerce may not have to be one in which conflict is endemic, corruption entrenched, ruthlessness and treachery commonplace. But, if that is how it is, how are you to survive in that world encumbered with moral virtues? In such a world, is it credible that moral virtues are still indispensable to your faring well? In order to function in such a world, do you not have to make compromises – be opportunist? While the theory that is virtues-based purports to latch on to universal truths about human nature and the human condition, doesn't it do so selectively, ignoring many unpalatable truths about human nature and the human condition that render the concerns of those who have virtues idealistic and foolish? Is this any wonder? Academic philosophers, who typically have no direct experience of earning a living outside the haven of their universities, may seem ill-qualified to produce moral theories that connect with the harsh realities of life in commerce – or public life; small wonder, then, if their theories have a 'fairy-tale quality'.[9]

Compare, in contrast, the 'rules-in-use' in business as elicited, for example, by Robert Jackall, a sociologist whose findings are based on first-hand field work – observation of the rules that actually do govern the behaviour of people in business and which those who get on in business have a clear grasp of.[10] I have argued (see chapter 6) that doing well in business is compatible with doing well in life – though doing well in life depends on having the moral virtues. But if doing well in business depends on following the rules-in-use described by Robert Jackall, how can I be right? He says, 'Mastering the subtle but necessary arts of deference without seeming to be deferential, and occasionally of the outright self-abasement such relationships require is a taxing endeavour that demands continual compromises with conventional and popular notions of integrity.'[11] And the rules-in-use that he observes do seem to suggest rather different priorities and concerns than those that I have ascribed to people who are humane and just. In the bureaucratic world, for example, he notes that what matters is not your willingness to stand by your actions but your agility to avoid blame; not what you stand for but whom you stand with.[12]

Of course, the complaint that ethics, as described by philosophers, is inapplicable in the real world – that philosophers seem out of touch – is hardly new. But it may seem particularly pertinent these days when some philosophers take it upon themselves to teach non-philosophers – for example, teaching business ethics to business people. The gist of the complaint is that these philosophers appear to be 'oblivious to the concrete business context and indifferent to the very particular role that people play in business.'[13]

Callicles upbraids Socrates for pursuing philosophical enquiries and neglecting to become worldly wise: 'Such men know nothing of the laws in their cities, or of the language they should use in their business associations both public and private with other men, or of human pleasures and appetites, and in a word they are completely without experience of men's characters. And so when they enter upon any activity public or private they appear ridiculous, just as public men, I suppose, appear ridiculous when they take part in your discussions and arguments.'[14] Callicles goes on to describe how Socrates, by his absorption in philosophical study, has made himself unfit to fend for himself or his friends: 'You neglect what you ought most to care for . . . you could neither contribute a useful word in the councils of justice nor seize upon what is plausible and convincing, nor offer any brilliant advice on another's behalf.'[15]

Thus Callicles derides the unrealism of Socrates: that Socrates ignores, for example, the relevance of might to right – that only those who lack might have reason to bother about right. In other words, contract-keeping, respecting rights, negotiating terms, only make sense, Callicles insists, between equals – among those who pose a threat to each other and who therefore stand to benefit by making a contract. You do not negotiate terms with animals – you do not need to:[16] they can be forced into servitude. So likewise, can some people be (e.g. outsiders) – as the Athenians tried to explain to the Melians, when Athens required the Melians to join their empire or be subjugated by it. The Melians wanted to talk about justice, the righteousness of their cause. The Athenians brushed aside such discussion: 'you know as well as we know that what is just is arrived at in human arguments only when the necessity on both sides is equal, and that the powerful exact what they can, while the weak yield what they must.'[17]

Needless to say, Socrates, is well aware of these 'realities' that Callicles appeals to. But Socrates claims to understand other realities that Callicles seems to ignore – truths about human nature and human needs, in the light of which it is evident that there is more to living well than wielding power. One needs wisdom as well as power. The kind of wisdom one needs is not a specialist knowledge, it is the kind of wisdom that involves emotional maturity and judgement – in short, the moral virtues. Socrates is concerned to work out what our priorities need to be if our lives are to go well – how, for example, a non-opportunistic attachment to virtues is essential for living well. If Socrates is right about this, then whether we are interested in defining what is ethically defensible in business or in medicine or in policing or whatever, we should start from an understanding of what are human virtues and why they matter.

The account of morality developed here is based on our understanding of the moral virtues that are essential for our living well. By definition, these virtues are just those traits of character that are indispensable for everyone everywhere to acquire – pervasively relevant and necessary. We cannot, then, bracket off the world of business and commerce, arguing that these virtues do not apply to how those who inhabit that world should act. That world, after all, is part of this world, and it supports on its back many of the good things of life that enable people to live well. Scholarship, science, technology, the arts, can only flourish in a culture which musters the means to support people who do not have to spend all their energies on surviving, who are provided for and protected by others who value their work. If a certain way of life is unethical, then depending on others to pursue that way of life is unethical. But being in business is not as such unethical, though being in some lines of business (drug-peddling, for example) is and though surviving or getting on in some business organizations is.

Is Jackall wrong, then, about the kind of demeanour and conduct that you need in order to do well in business: for example, that you should pander to the bosses, laugh at their jokes, leave your convictions at home, generally avoid 'making waves' and make sure that you are always on the winning side? Do you have to fit in with these rules only in *some* organizations? Or, if Jackall is right to suggest that these rules *characterize* commercial organizations generally, is it, even so, possible to come to terms with these rules in a way that is honourable, that does not compromise the principles of those who have virtues? We will explore this latter possibility.

Honourable Compromises

Is it possible for people who are humane and just, who have principles, to fit in to, and get on in, organizations of the type Jackall describes? Let us pick up on one of the necessary strategies he mentions, which on the face of it would present problems: social distancing – the importance of knowing how to drop a colleague who falls out of organizational favour – whether deservedly or undeservedly.[18] Is this kind of behaviour compatible with humanity? What if the colleague in question happens to be a good friend – do you not have a duty to stand by your colleague, to show loyalty? Jackall quotes from a 'high-ranking staff official': 'Anxiety is endemic to anyone who works in a corporation. By the time you get to middle management, it's difficult to make friends because the normal requirement for friendship – that is, *loyalty* – doesn't fit in this context. You have to look out for number one more than anything else.'[19]

Now, it is not necessarily unethical for a business organization to discourage or restrict those with whom you are allowed to make friends. In professions, too, it may be appropriate to require that members avoid making friends with certain others: that teachers are cautioned against making friends with individual pupils, social workers about making friends with clients and nurses about making friends with patients. A distancing that friendship undermines may be necessary if one is to do one's job properly. But, of course, maintaining that distance does not mean that you are unfriendly, uncivil or lacking in compassion. But if avoiding forming certain friendships is a requirement of the organization you are in, then you and others in the organization, if you observe the rule, will not be required to be 'disloyal' to those who fall out of favour. The question of loyalty should not arise. You are advised not to form friendships so that you do not get trapped into just such predicaments. All the same, if the organization requires both that you avoid making friends with colleagues and that you put in a 12-hour day in their midst then there is, surely, a problem over pursuing the concerns of those who have virtues and getting on in the organization. If work-time pretty well uses up all one's waking time, one must be able to pursue all of the virtue-related concerns *in* one's work.

It is easy for outside observers to misunderstand the culture of an organization, to suppose, for example, that levity among those whose work is highly stressful shows lack of sensitivity or seriousness, whereas it may be the most effective, least disruptive, way of their handling the stress they are under – stress that they only feel because they are sensitive and serious. Similarly, we might misinterpret the careful distance-keeping of professionals or business people in their work.

The account of morality that we have developed in this book emphasizes the difference between how constraint-type obligations and how aspirational-type obligations bind. If we do not pay attention to this difference, we are likely to exaggerate the demands of morality and to assume wrongly that you cannot get on in business unless you are prepared to cast aside or compromise principles, to leave your virtues at home. It need not be so. As we have seen, the justice-related virtues involve a primary concern not ourselves to act unjustly – largely, a matter of 'negative' duties – and a secondary concern to promote justice in the world – for example, by stopping others from acting unjustly. The duties relating to both these concerns bind, but differently. The duty you are under not to cheat your employees applies *vis-à-vis* all your employees – those overseas no less than those here at home. You cannot pick and choose whom not to cheat. But your duty to stop others acting unjustly does allow you to pick and choose – except, of course, if you have taken on special obligations to stop certain injustices – as if you are a policeman, or an accountant hired to investigate a suspected fraud. Your duty to prevent injustice does allow you to pick and choose – special obligations aside – provided the overall pattern of how you do so is consistent with your really caring that justice be done.

Hence, it would be a mistake to see every missed opportunity to prevent an injustice being done as automatically, unprincipled compromise. You might genuinely care about justice yet routinely turn a blind eye to some instances of injustice at work that you are in a position (or think you are) to stop. Maybe you are aware of how some of your colleagues embellish in small ways their expense claims – it may be part of the tradition in this organization to do so – and yet you do not interfere because it is a minor injustice and the commotion of putting a stop to it seems unwarranted. Where what is at issue is how far and in what way to pursue a virtue-related concern, the language of balancing concerns and weighing consequences is entirely in order – and need not involve dishonourable compromise. To decide to keep silent about the trivial injustice rather than to 'make waves' may be both sensible and consistent with your having a real commitment to justice. But the duties relating to the primary concern not to act unjustly oneself should not be seen similarly just as considerations to be weighed alongside other considerations. The expectation of those who have virtues needs to be that they conduct their lives at work and off work within certain constraints.

Yet we have also seen that sometimes we face dilemmas – situations in which it appears that we cannot or should not act within the constraints – whether because the constraints themselves seem to be tugging us in different directions or because conforming to the constraints in the situation means forgoing a special opportunity to prevent harm or do good. Dilemmas, we have said, must be resolvable in a principled way. But they are not always easy to resolve – even for those who have virtues. The correct resolution of a dilemma is not a dishonourable compromise.

Suppose that you have promised to deliver supplies to a company on a certain day – and you understand that the company is counting on you to do so: the supplies are urgently needed. A sudden snow storm might make driving conditions so difficult that you decide to cancel: you weigh up the risk or stress your driver delivering would be subject to and decide it is not justified. In the circumstances, the decision not to keep your promise may be a justifiable accommodation – not an unprincipled compromise, not a failure to be true to your word. Your promise to deliver by a certain date must not be understood as a commitment to do so regardless of the cost to yourself or others.

The need to accommodate, to compromise, in resolving dilemmas is not peculiar to business. Dilemmas arise no less for scholars, policemen, journalists or charity workers than for people in business – though the types of dilemmas that arise may differ depending on which field one is in. Thus, the mere fact that you regularly have to compromise between competing claims in business does not put in doubt the possibility of being principled and being in business.

Not only is it possible to be in business and be principled, it is also possible to be in business and lead a morally exemplary life, pursuing admirable ideals and keeping within the constraints of morality in one's day to day working life – in how one makes choices and shapes policies on the job. There is nothing more problematic about a businessperson fully participating in and contributing to the good life than about the doctor or scholar doing so. People in business who are morally admirable will demonstrate by the way they do business how ethical constraints *and* aspirations can both be integrated into life in business. They will keep within the justice-related constraints in how they do business and they will find how their business activities open up opportunities for furthering their ethical aspirations: that is part of what makes their way of doing business distinctive – not just what they won't do but what they will do and how they go about doing it.

The supposition that if you are in business your virtues are bound to be compromised derives not from feet-on-the-ground realism about the demands of business but from misunderstanding of the demands of virtues. As we have seen, for example, it is not necessarily unreasonable to require employees to avoid striking up certain friendships. Requiring them to avoid incurring the duties of loyalty is not the same as requiring them to be disloyal. Nor does it belie the claim that loyalty is a moral virtue and hence relevant in all contexts. It is because it is relevant in all contexts that it may be necessary to be circumspect in the friendships you form at work lest you incur obligations that you cannot fulfil in view of other obligations you have taken on.

Similarly, generosity is a virtue but it is not *ungenerous* of chief executives of commercial companies to refuse to donate money to worthy causes. The money has been entrusted to them for other purposes. As R.E. Ewin observes (echoing Elaine Sternberg), 'What is characteristic of commercial companies, as opposed to charities or churches, is that they exist to make money for their shareholders.'[20] And 'there is nothing generous or charitable in giving away what is someone else's'.[21] The point is not that chief executives are entitled to be ungenerous, but that they are not in a position where they can be generous: giving away what is not yours to give is not *being* generous.

R.E. Ewin and Elaine Sternberg both contend that certain virtues are needed in some contexts and not in others. In business, they contend that it is the justice-related virtues that are needed – the most important virtue, according to Ewin, being honesty. I have argued, though, that (cardinal) moral virtues are pervasively relevant. Thus, while I agree with Ewin and Sternberg that the chief executive of a commercial company is not able to be generous by giving away other people's money, I maintain that if generosity is a virtue then chief executives need to have it and their having it should make a difference to how they act in their business role. To explain how, one would need to pursue further what generosity means, what makes it a virtue – and not merely a minor virtue: it will presumably have to involve more than offering money to help those in need. It will explain what character trait, what attitude, underlies that kind of manifestation of generosity and other manifestations – like, maybe, a willingness sometimes to relax terms, to drive fair bargains but not the hardest bargain the law allows, to compete keenly, but not losing sight of the humanity of one's opponents.

The Starting Point for Business Ethics

In order to address the particular problems and issues that relate to business ethics, one needs a grasp of what being ethical involves and why it matters. This we have sought to explain through our study of the notion of moral virtues, of what these are and why we need them. Only if these virtues are, as I have claimed, necessary for all of us to pursue and incorporate into all aspects of our lives, does it make sense to draw up a map that everyone needs to refer to.

The possibility of producing such a map – useful to people in all walks of life, in different societies, with different or no religious beliefs, of different talents, with different personalities and attitudes – may be challenged. Does everyone have enough in common, that we can confidently point them to the one map? What we do have in common is the need to achieve lives worth living and the potential we all have to better our chances through the cultivation of virtues of character. The virtues of character each of us needs are the same just because we all need to acquire sensitivity and judgement in respect of our emotions – for example: fear, anger, curiosity, love, pride.

It may be argued that the only virtue that everyone needs is the virtue of justice, that the other virtues may be more or less important depending on the kind of culture one lives in and one's own particular way of life. Thus, for example, Stuart Hampshire suggests that courage may be dispensable for some, as justice cannot be: 'there could be a scholarly and withdrawn way of life, with its supporting virtues, which would only in very exceptional circumstances require acts of courage: not so for justice, always required'.[22]

But isn't this plausible only if one defines the virtue of courage as well-judged mastery of fear in situations where one is threatened *physically*? We might call that 'valour' rather than 'courage': valour, then, would be courage on the battlefield or in the bull-ring, a minor virtue just in that one could expect to get by in life without it, whereas courage as such, surely, must be a cardinal virtue since everyone needs to cope with fear (if not in the bull-ring, maybe in the board-room or in the ball-room).[23] In other words, to understand how courage can be a cardinal virtue one must understand it quite simply as well-judged mastery of fear. We encounter many fearful situations where we are not physically threatened – academics, no less than other people: the fear of the mockery or scorn of one's academic colleagues; the fear that one might not be sufficiently intelligent or lucky to find through one's researches anything new to say that is worth saying. It takes courage to face criticism honestly and openly and to resist the temptation to fend it off with ridicule, lies or self-deception. It takes courage to admit you were wrong and to apologize. If you are drafted to go to war, you may be able to hire someone else to take your place, but you cannot achieve a worthwhile life without learning to control your own fears and to develop judgement in what you find fearful and in how you handle your fears.

While the virtue of justice, understood to cover no more than acceptance of the basic constraints that enable people to live in peace, negotiating terms rather than using force to impose their wills, is undeniably necessary in any society – a precondition of living cooperatively – I have argued that other virtues are necessary too, for two reasons: (1) because commitment to justice is too fragile unless it is underpinned by other virtues – cowards may not want to lie but be too scared to tell the truth; the dissolute may mean well but lack the firmness of character to keep their word; and (2) because even if the virtue of justice could stand alone, the kind of life we could enjoy if we had only this virtue would not yet be a life worth living – we need to have justice to be able to pursue our aspirations, but we also need to have aspirations and ones that do not turn out to be hollow. In order to find such aspirations and pursue them effectively we need other virtues besides justice: 'The sense of justice makes human life possible, and the other virtues make it worthwhile.'[24]

Yet do we all need the *same* virtues? Does it not make a difference whether, for example, we have religious beliefs, and if we do, which religious beliefs, to what aspirations we have and what virtues – apart from justice – we need to acquire? Machiavelli and Nietzsche propose a different set of virtues from the virtues extolled in Christianity. As Hampshire observes, from a religious point of view, one might single out as virtues 'absolute integrity, gentleness, disposition to sympathy, a fastidious sense of honour, generosity, a disposition to gratitude', whereas from a more worldly Machiavellian point of view, one might rather single out such qualities as 'tenacity and resolution, courage in the face of risk, intelligence, largeness of design and purpose, exceptional energy, habits of leadership'.[25] And surely, in writing references for students applying for jobs in marketing, in commerce, one would not expect that ascribing the former set of qualities to them would lead to their being short-listed, whereas ascribing the latter set might well do so. You might be quite pleased to discover that your future son-in-law had the former qualities but they are perhaps not quite what you look for when choosing a lawyer to fight your corner or a manager to market a new product.

All the same, I stand by the conception of moral virtues as necessary for everyone regardless of their religious views, if any, of their cultural background, their social circumstances, their personal ambitions: 'Whatever happiness may be, and however it differs from person to person, there are certain essential if variable personal ingredients that are required. We can summarise them in a single word, in the concept of the *virtues*.'[26] I have said that in order to be just in character, you need other virtues. You need courage, tenacity and resolution, intelligence – Machiavellian virtues. But these virtues, though necessary, are hardly sufficient. They do not take the place of justice. Though you want your lawyer or manager to be tough, resilient and energetic, you may not be too pleased if you find that he does not keep his word to you, or if his ruthlessness and lack of sympathy come out in how he treats you and the projects that are dear to you.

But is it really possible for someone to combine all these qualities: to be both gentle and tough, energetic and fastidious in matters of honour? Gentleness is not a virtue except it is gentleness where gentleness is appropriate. Likewise, with tenacity – it has to be tenacity about the right things in the right way on the right occasion – for example, tenacity in resisting bribes, in being true to your word. Tenacity about the wrong things in the wrong ways is a kind of stubbornness or obstinacy, which reduces one's effectiveness as a negotiator or manager. In short, none of these qualities counts as a moral virtue except it is combined with sensitivity and judgement.

Robert Solomon observes: 'Except for a relatively small number of very specialised and autonomous managerial tasks, almost all organisational duties – and their success or failure – depend upon our personal relations with other people.'[27] What determines our competence on this front is nothing other than our moral virtues or lack of them: anyone who has the Machiavellian virtues and not the Christian (as listed above) or the Christian but not the Machiavellian will not be liked or trusted. If you are gentle but have no mettle, you are a weak support to your colleagues in times of difficulty, you are unreliable – a pushover, however amiable. If you are tenacious but lack sympathy you will irritate and annoy; people may use you and drop you as soon as they think that they can get by without you.

It follows that everyone needs the virtues. But it does not follow that everyone needs to share some agreed goal as the object of morality. We can pursue our very different ways of life and demonstrate the same virtues in pursuance of them. Yet in order to be able to do so effectively, we do need to have some shared understanding, some appreciation of how different ways of life afford opportunities and challenges for those who have virtues. Especially, do we need this understanding in regard to those with whom, or for whom, we work – those with whom we have to agree policies or whose policies it is our job to carry out. Hence, the importance of dialogue, of being able to explain and to seek explanation without those whose explanations are sought taking umbrage. Where what is in question is the ethical appropriateness of a policy – whether it is consistent with good practice – we need some procedure for ethical review. The procedure here proposed is reference to our map: it is our reference point. So what does it tell us?

First of all, it differentiates among our obligations, distinguishing constraint-type from aspiration-type. The former show up on the map as no-go or restricted access areas. The latter show up as areas that we keep within reach of. Secondly, this still leaves us considerable room, but how much room depends on our particular circumstances: where we are starting from, how we are travelling – whether we have acquired special obligations that make some areas no-go for ourselves which are not no-go for everybody, or whether we have taken on special responsibilities that oblige us to venture into what is a no-go area for most people but is not, in the circumstances, for ourselves.

The Map and its Limitations

The practical aim of business ethics – and the aim of this enquiry – is to establish what is good practice in business. To this end we have sketched a map. The map is not complete. The map is, after all, just a map of morality with no more relevance (and no less) for people in business than for people in politics, in teaching or in the police service. The map, then, does not by itself answer all our questions concerning what is good practice in business. It is, all the same, the necessary starting point and reference point.

The basic map provides a framework. The framework will already rule out some practices, which may include some that are accepted, that are the rules-in-use in some organizations. But the map may need further details to be filled in, by those with appropriate knowledge and experience, if it is to give guidance on issues in business that are ethically complex and controversial. The filling in of detail, what details need filling in and how it is done will depend on the needs and aims of those concerned – not just whether they are in business as against in journalism but, if they are in business, the kind of business it is, the kind of problems encountered.

Because the relevant contextual information will vary from business to business, and within a business over time, the map may be differently filled in by different parties without one filling in necessarily being *better* than another. Furthermore, the map will need continuing review and updating as circumstances change. What should remain the same and untampered with is the basic framework, the framework that everyone needs to work from and preserve, whether in business or not. In a sense, then, what is good practice in business never changes: good practice respects the basic framework; in another sense, there can be a variety of alternative good practices, none of which redraws the map but each of which fills it in differently.

Mission Accomplished?

An introduction to business ethics should explain both why and how: why study of business ethics matters – especially why it matters for people in business – and how to do it. Does the study matter – for people in business? Only, surely, if it teaches them something they do not know already and something that they need to know.

They do not know already. Not, of course, that the answers are not often obvious. There are, though, in business and out of it, situations where it is not clear what rules to apply or how they apply. Getting it right (that is, not getting it wrong) on such occasions requires *study* – beyond just consulting one's own or other people's consciences. While it is always wrong to do what you think is wrong, it is not always all right to do what you (or other people) think is all right – what you or 'we' feel comfortable doing. Quite possibly most Britons did not feel uncomfortable about the policy of unstrategic bombing of German cities in 1945. But a survey of opinion could tell us nothing about the ethical defensibility of such a policy. It would only tell us what people thought to be defensible – another matter altogether.

Do people in business need to know what is ethically defensible or indefensible practice in business? Obviously, they need to know what is *thought* to be indefensible – especially these days. Anne McElvoy, commenting in *The Spectator* on the new phenomenon of ethical consumerism, observes, 'As consumers, producers and traders, we are undergoing an ethical boom in which morality has become the latest commodity in the market place.'[28] In the present climate, businesses are likely to be called to account for what are *perceived* failings and, whether the public's perceptions are fair or unfair, their effect on a business can be disastrous. Is this consumer interest in the ethical profile of businesses – for example, in how actively businesses support good causes – something that those in business, who have virtues and the related concerns, can be expected to welcome? Not necessarily. Being active is not the same as being effective. Those who have the virtue-related concerns will not confuse the appearance of do-gooding with the reality. They may even find that focus on appearances gets in the way of acting well.

While everyone understands the pragmatic need to 'sing whatever song the client wants to hear', as Jackall puts it,[29] commitment to ethically defensible practice in business cannot be based just on that need. Not all clients are concerned to avoid wrongdoing, nor are those who are concerned always aware of what doings are wrong. Our account of what morality is about, why we all need virtues, explains why it matters that we do what is ethically defensible and not just what is thought to be so by ourselves and those around us.

How, then, do we work out what is ethically defensible or indefensible in business? Our starting point and continuing reference point, our map, is based on our understanding of what virtues we need in order to achieve lives worth living. By study of these virtues and the concerns they involve, we can compose a map that at least marks off danger areas and areas to keep within reach of. To understand the map one needs to engage in philosophical study: analysing basic concepts such as good and bad, right and wrong, the concept of virtues and the nature of particular virtues – what these involve and why they matter.

To use the map in a particular context one may need to fill in more detail, and doing that may require information and under-standing of a contextual sort. This is the sort of information and understanding that people in business can bring to bear on morally problematic business practices or policies. But their wisdom is not by itself adequate to resolve what is morally complex unless they also have a grasp of the map. Hence the value of dialogue between those who understand the map and those who understand the context. Hence, especially, the value of those in business them-selves reflecting on the map.

Further Reading

On applied ethics
See Winkler and Coombs, *Applied Ethics*; Almond, *Introducing Applied Ethics*.

On compromises, honourable or dishonourable
See Williams, *Moral Luck*; and Nagel, 'Ruthlessness in public life'.

On virtues in business
See Shaw, 'Virtues for a postmodern world'; Nesteruk, 'Law and the virtues'; Boatright, 'Aristotle meets Wall Street'; and Ewin, 'The virtues appropriate to business'. See also Solomon, 'Business ethics'.

Study Questions

1 Suppose that unless you fall in with the practice of your colleagues and inflate your expenses in the same way they do, you will be exposing them to censure, is it indefensible for you to fall in line? Does it make any difference whether the sums of money involved are trifling? Justify your answer.
2 Manuel Velasquez (1995) reports that the aluminium companies operating in Jamaica in the 1960s and 1970s 'gave impoverished

and underdeveloped Jamaica the bottom-most dregs of the processing stages of this highly profitable industry.'[30]

Do you consider this to be ethically indefensible? Justify your answer.

3   Find some examples of honourable and of dishonourable compromises in business practice and explain your choices. Is the decision to expel the Saudi dissident, Mohammed Masari (see study question 4, chapter 7) an example of an honourable or dishonourable compromise?

4   Anne McElvoy suggests that 'there are disquieting overtones' in the business fashion for 'corporate citizenship': 'What say do the shareholders or customers have in the type of environmentalism or ethics that are embraced? Precious little.'[31]

Do you agree that there is this reason, or other reasons, for disquiet about this fashion? Can you instance any cases where well-intentioned promoting of a good cause by a business has had untoward consequences? If so, what lessons would you draw?

Notes

Introduction

1 Seth, *A Suitable* Boy, especially pp. 913–27 (sections 13.26–13.29) and pp. 1111–20 (sections 16.8–16.10).
2 Iago in Shakespeare's *Othello*, I.iii.
3 Sternberg, *Just Business*; cf. Warnock, *The Object of Morality*, ch. 2 'The human predicament'; Hart, *The Concept of Law*, pp. 190–5.

Chapter 2   Doing Right

1 The following three sections were first published in 1992 in 'Coming to ethical terms: right and wrong', in *Business Ethics: A European Review*, 1, 154–6, and are reprinted here with minor modifications by kind permission of the editor and publisher.
2 See the extended and insightful development of the analogy between chess rules and moral rules in Denyer, 'Chess and life'.
3 Hobbes, *Leviathan*, p. 97.
4 We will come back to this topic, for there is more to be said regarding reasons for not taking advantage of those over whom one has power, in ch. 4.
5 Hampshire, *Innocence and* Experience, p. 90.

Chapter 3   Doing Well

1 The following three sections were first published in 1992 in 'Coming to ethical terms: good and bad', in *Business Ethics: A European Review*, 1, 211–12, and are reprinted here with minor modifications by kind permission of the editor and publisher.

2   This point about the meaning of good, and the further points made in this subsection are derived from Geach, 'Good and evil'.
3   Aristotle, *The Nicomachean Ethics*, book I.
4   Foot, 'Goodness and choice'.
5   From *Production Engineer*, 1975, 1(54), 2; quoted by Harris, 'Professional codes', p. 105.
6   This example is taken from Foot, 'Moral realism'.
7   For a full discussion of the moral significance of this distinction, see Foot, 'The problem of abortion'.

Chapter 4   *Motives, Moral Reasons and Compliance*

1   More accurately, as danger areas – these areas are no-go for most of us most of the time but some of us may come under special obligations which necessitate or allow us to make some incursions into these areas.
2   Hume, *Enquiry*, section IX, part II, pp. 282–3.
3   See Plato, *Republic*, pp. 44 ff.
4   See Foot, *Virtues and Vices*, p. 3.
5   See Singer, *How Are We to Live?*, p. 205. In ch. 6 it will be argued that a lack of temperance can be shown by unreasonable self-denial as well as by excessive self-indulgence.
6   See Jackall, *Moral Mazes*, pp. 91 ff.
7   *Ibid.*, p. 92.
8   *Ibid.*, p. 94.
9   Hume, *A Treatise*, book III, part II, section ii, p. 490.
10 Reggie von Zubach, in a letter to *The Times*, 17 March 1990.
11 Carmichael and Drummond, *Good Business*, p. 74.
12 Shakespeare's *Othello*, I.iii.
13 On 'the loss of community', see Singer, *How Are We to Live?*, pp. 28–37.
14 Hosmer, *The Ethics of Management*, p. 178, commenting on the Exxon Valdez case.
15 *Ibid.*, p. 181.

Chapter 5   *Virtues for Life*

1   See Hart *The Concept of Law*, pp. 190–5.
2   See Warnock, *The Object of Morality*, ch. 2.
3   *Ibid.*, pp. 190–1.
4   *Ibid.*, p. 191.
5   Hume, *A Treatise*, book III, part II.

6   Foot, *Virtues and Vices*, p. 8; cf. Aristotle, *The Nicomachean Ethics*, VI.5, p. 143, 1140b.

7   Russell, *A History*, p. 196.

8   Aristotle, *The Nicomachean Ethics*, II.6, p. 39, 1107a.

9   Stuart Hampshire suggests that courage is not something that we all need, that we can hire others to be courageous for us. See *Innocence and Experience*, p. 72. I will come back to this suggestion in ch. 11.

10 Geach, *The Virtues*, p. 13.

11 On compassion, see Blum, 'Compassion', pp. 507–17.

12 Nietzsche: 'He who has a why to live for can bear almost any how'. Quoted by Frankl in *Man's Search for Meaning*, p. 67, in regard to his experience of concentration camp life.

13 Betty Friedan, quoted by Singer in *How Are We to Live?*, p. 198.

14 Aristotle, *The Nicomachean Ethics*, IV.6, p. 99, 1126b.

15 Arguably, there cannot be a secular analogue to charity. Peter Geach treats charity as essentially a theological virtue: 'love of men that does not flow from love of God may be an agreeable thing enough, but it is only part of a fashion of this world that passes away, and we should not overvalue it', *The Virtues*, p. 81.

16 Aristotle, *The Nicomachean Ethics*, VIII, 1154.

17 *Ibid.*, VIII, 1154.

18 Lord Goring in Oscar Wilde's *An Ideal Husband*, II.

19 Aristotle does not, it seems, recognize humanity as a virtue. Friendship on his account involves only those towards whom you have a prior commitment. As Julia Annas observes, concern for 'the furthest Mysian' is no part of Aristotle's conception of what you need to achieve a life worth living. See Annas, *Morality and Happiness*, p. 224, cf. p. 250. Aristotle does, though, seem to recognize *friendliness* to be a virtue: 'But the state in question differs from friendship in that it implies no passion or affection for one's associates; since it is not by reason of loving or hating that such a man takes everything in the right way, but by being a man of a certain kind. For he will behave so alike towards those he knows and those he does not know, towards intimates and those who are not so, except that in each of these cases he will behave as is befitting; for it is not proper to have the same care for strangers, nor again is it the same conditions that make it right to give pain to them', *The Nicomachean Ethics*, IV.6, p. 99, 1126b.

20 The following three sections were first published in 1992 in 'Coming to ethical terms: motive and morality', in *Business Ethics: A European Review*, 1, 264–6, and are reprinted here with minor modifications by kind permission of the editor and publisher.

21   See Hobbes, *Leviathan*, p. 116.
22   'It is natural for me to leave you and my earthly rulers without any feeling of grief or bitterness, since I believe I shall find there, no less than here, good rulers and good friends', quoted in Plato's 'Phaedo', p. 116, St 69e.
23   Weil, *Seventy Letters*, p. 20.
24   *Ibid.*, pp. 20–22.

Chapter 6   *Reconciling Business Life with Moral Virtues*

1   This chapter is a substantially revised version of my paper, 'Reconciling business imperatives and moral virtues', in *Introducing Applied Ethics*, edited by Brenda Almond, Blackwell, Oxford, 1995, and is reprinted here with the kind permission of the editor and publisher.
2   Geach, *The Virtues*, p. 131.
3   *Ibid.*, p. 16.
4   Plato, *Republic*, p. 7, St 330d; cf. 'it is impossible, or not easy, to do noble deeds without the proper equipment. In many actions we use friends and riches and political power as instruments' in Aristotle, *The Nicomachean Ethics*, p. 17, 1099a.
5   Galbraith, *The Affluent Society*.
6   As we have already noted, Peter Geach maintains that charity is essentially a theological concept – 'to be prized only if there is a God. The word "charity" bears other senses, but it is dubious whether in these other senses charity is a virtue at all', Geach, *The Virtues*, p. 17; cf. p. 81.
7   On this see Mill, 'Utilitarianism', ch. 5.
8   Of course, duties may be clearly fulfillable and yet allow more or less scope for how and when they are fulfilled; for example, your promise to deliver supplies 'this week' does not commit you to a particular day or hour.
9   See ch. 11 for further consideration of compromise, of the possibility of honourable compromise, compromise that is consistent with virtues.
10   Mill, 'Utilitarianism', ch. 5.
11   But not always. Someone who is honest may see fit to lie in some special circumstances – so I shall argue.
12   On the motivation of those who have the virtue, Hobbes says: 'That which gives to humane actions the relish of justice, is a certain noblenesse or gallantnesse of courage (rarely found,) by which a man scorns to be beholding for the contentment of his life, to fraud or breach of promise', *Leviathan*, p. 114.

13   Marx, *Capital*, vol.1, preface, p. 21.
14   'The term "trustworthy" can be used to refer to the general commit-
     ment to be worthy of the trust of one's fellow human beings, and
     this form of conscientiousness is the genus of which fairness, honesty,
     truthfulness, and being a person of one's word are all the more
     specific forms.' Wallace, *Virtues and Vices*, p. 109.
15   Not that those who show a virtue on a given occasion do so *in order
     to* be useful or agreeable thereby.
16   Hume, *Enquiry*, p. 270, section 219. In fairness to monks, though,
     should we not allow that if their theological views are to be taken
     seriously, their monkish virtues may after all be mighty useful if not
     agreeable? Consider, for instance, the idea that one might be able to
     aid others by offering up hardship one voluntarily submitted to – as
     Christ died, for others.
17   Joanne Cuilla discusses the scope for 'creative' thinking to resolve
     moral dilemmas in business: 'the really creative part of business
     ethics is discovering ways to do what is morally right and socially
     responsible without ruining your career and company. Sometimes
     such creativity requires being like the cartoon mouse who outsmarts
     the cat.' See Cuilla, 'Business ethics', p. 215.
18   Hume, *Enquiry*, section 219.
19   Aristotle, *The Nicomachean Ethics*, section 1119a.
20   Plato, 'Phaedo', 68c ff.
21   Reported by Singer, *How Are We to Live?*, pp. 205–6.
22   *Ibid.*, p. 206.
23   Hayek, 'The non sequitur', pp. 363–6.
24   As Ewin points out in 'The virtues appropriate to business',
     pp. 834–5.
25   See, for example, Pappworth, *Human Guinea Pigs*.
26   Sternberg, *Just Business*, p. 106.
27   Carr, 'Is business bluffing ethical?', p. 321.
28   Solomon, *Ethics and Excellence*, ch. 5.
29   Geach, *The Virtues*.

Chapter 7   Role Duties

1   See ch. 3, p. 37.
2   See Graham, 'The registrar in the John Lewis Partnership', pp. 185–
    91.
3   Shakespeare's *King Lear*, I.i.
4   Published in LIA's magazine, *Prospect,* and reported in *The Sunday
    Times*, 10 December 1995.

5 Sternberg, *Just Business*, p. 196.
6 Hosmer, *The Ethics of Management*, p. 27.
7 *Ibid.*, p. 29.
8 Report by Andrew Lorenz in *The Sunday Times*, 21 January 1996.

Chapter 8 Good Practice in Business

1 See ch. 1.
2 See Smart and Williams, *Utilitarianism*, pp. 93–100.
3 In so far as deontologists merely point up the failings of utilitarianism, they are not offering a rival theory.
4 See Rawls, *A Theory of Justice*, pp. 22–7.
5 Arthur Miller's *Death of a Salesman*, I.
6 *Ibid.*, II.
7 See Sorell and Hendry, *Business Ethics*, pp. 19–22.
8 Freeman, *Strategic Management*, p. vi.
9 I take this phrase from Elaine Sternberg, who uses it to define the aim of (commercial) business – to maximize long-term owner value by selling goods or services. See Sternberg, *Just Business*, pp. 42–56, for her explanation of why this phrase captures more accurately what (commercial) business is about than other common alternatives.
10 *Ibid.*, p. 79.
11 *Ibid.*, p. 79.
12 Sorell and Hendry, *Business Ethics*, p. 21.
13 Solomon, 'Business ethics', pp. 360–1.
14 McCracken and Shaw, 'Virtue ethics and contractarianism', p. 301.

Chapter 9 Good Practice in the Firm

1 Sternberg, *Just Business*, p. 37.
2 *Ibid.*, p. 37.
3 *Ibid.*, p. 124.
4 See Health and Safety at Work etc. Act 1974, s. 2(1).
5 See Ian Birrell and Grace Bradberry, 'Toyota orders drug tests on workers at new British plants', *The Sunday Times*, 13 October 1995, p. 1 of section 3.
6 See 'Du Pont's policy of exclusion from the workplace' in Beauchamp, *Case Studies*, pp. 33–8.
7 See Coplon, 'When did Johns-Manville know?', pp. 98–100.
8 See Donaldson, *The Ethics of International Business*, p. 127.
9 Vallance, *Business Ethics at Work*, p. 70.
10 Sorell and Hendry, *Business Ethics*, p. 85.

11 *Ibid.*, p. 85.
12 Sternberg, *Just Business*, p. 131.
13 *Ibid.*, p. 55.
14 *Ibid.*, pp. 200–201.
15 Compare Ewin, 'The virtues appropriate to business', who argues that business does not have a purpose as such. He is happy to allow, though, that commercial business 'exists for the sake of making profits for its shareholders', p. 835.
16 See Sternberg, 'Teleology and business ethics'.
17 See Coope, 'Justice and jobs', pp. 71–7, for a more thorough critique of the presumption that justice requires that the most competent candidate be chosen.
18 *Ibid.*, p. 74.
19 Ewin, 'The virtues appropriate to business', p. 841, also deprecates the 'Robin Hood operations' by executives who succumb to the temptation to 'cut a good figure'.
20 Sternberg, *Just Business*, p. 145.

Chapter 10   Good Practice outside the Firm

1 See Tamari, *In the Marketplace*, p. 119. Tamari adds: 'Banks place the same emphasis on the debtor's financial reports, profitability and future viability as do investors. In the case of large lenders, they may often behave as shareholders, demanding a seat or a nominee on the board of directors. In many economies, such as Japan and Israel, the share of assets represented by loan capital is greater than the owner's equity, making the creditor, in effect, an owner, if not in the legal sense, then at least in the commercial one.'
2 See Ewin, 'The virtues appropriate to business', p. 834.
3 To be precise, we should add 'or threat to trust'. Normally, only abuses of trust are threats to trust. But if your actions are perceived by others, rightly or wrongly, to be an abuse of trust, they will undermine trust.
4 See Strudler, 'On the ethics of deception', p. 820.
5 See the response to Strudler by Dees and Cramton, 'Deception and mutual trust'.
6 *Ibid.*
7 Strudler, 'On the ethics of deception', p. 818.
8 Of course, the legal duty is created in response to an underlying moral duty which those who have the virtue-related concerns acknowledge – for example, the duty to help the poor. But that duty does not have to be pursued through taxation and may be pursued independently of it.

9   Sebastian Hamilton in *The Sunday Times*, 31 December 1995, p. 1 of section 5.

10   Compare the attitude of Ford in launching its Pinto car although the management knew that its petrol tank was dangerous: the fact that Ford was complying with existing legislation (in 1968) is ethically irrelevant.

11   'It would be grossly unfair, if legislators would not make rules governing certain sorts of business behaviour, if one company were expected to put itself at a competitive disadvantage by limiting itself in some way in which others were not limited. If the behaviour is such that the company should not undertake it, then the legislators should keep the competition fair by placing the limitation on all. That way, the national interest is protected and the nation as a whole, rather than just that company, bears the burden of protecting it, paying higher prices in order to do so rather than putting that company at risk of going out of business.' Ewin, 'The virtues appropriate to business', p. 837.

12   See Sternberg, *Just Business*.

13   Reported in 'Truths, half-truths and insurance patter', *The Sunday Times*, 10 December 1995.

14   Hosmer, *The Ethics of Management*, p. 27.

15   Reported by Maurice Chittenden and Edward Welsh in 'Customers misled in scramble for bargains', *The Sunday Times*, 24 December 1989.

16   Solomon, *Ethics and Excellence*, p. 237.

Chapter 11   Virtues, the Key to Good Practice

1   See Velasquez, 'International business ethics'.

2   *Ibid.*, p. 875.

3   *Ibid.*, p. 875.

4   See Donaldson, *The Ethics of International Business*.

5   See Velasquez, 'International business ethics', p. 879.

6   Shown on Granada Television on 8 January 1996.

7   And is suing Granada Television for libel.

8   Marcus Sieff explains how the firm makes sure that all its suppliers conform to the same standards of good relations with employees in *Management the Marks & Spencer Way*, p. 1. He further observes that 'all workers should be given the same consideration as human beings. The young sales person and the senior stores manager are as human beings equal, and should be treated so.' (p. 95).

9   Hampshire, *Innocence and Experience*, p. 12.

10   See Jackall, *Moral Mazes*.
11   *Ibid.*, p. 203.
12   *Ibid.*, p. 193.
13   Solomon, *Ethics and Excellence*, p. 99.
14   In Plato, *Gorgias*, St 484–6.
15   *Ibid.*, St 486.
16   With the notable exception of George in Alan Ayckbourn's *Absurd Persons Singular*.
17   Thucydides, *History of the Peloponnesian War*, book V.
18   Jackall, *Moral Mazes*, p. 39. Cf. 'In fact, when it is even suspected that a person might be headed for trouble, anticipatory avoidance is the rule. Since one never knows what standards or criteria might be invoked to determine fates, it certainly makes little sense to be associated with those whose career threads seem already to be measured for cutting.' (p. 68).
19   *Ibid.*, p. 69.
20   Ewin, 'The virtues appropriate to business', p. 837.
21   *Ibid.*, p. 838.
22   Hampshire, *Innocence and Experience*, p. 72.
23   See Cordner, 'Aristotelian virtue', p. 301.
24   Ewin, *Co-operation and Human Values*, p. 161.
25   Hampshire, *Innocence and Experience*, p. 177.
26   Solomon, *Ethics and Excellence*, p. 107.
27   *Ibid.*, p. 130.
28   McElvoy, 'The moral daze', p. 9.
29   Jackall, *Moral Mazes*, p. 183.
30   Velasquez, 'International business ethics', p. 867.
31   McElvoy, 'The moral daze', p. 10.

Bibliography

Almond, Brenda (ed.), *Introducing Applied Ethics*, Oxford, Blackwell, 1995.

Annas, Julia, *Morality and Happiness*, New York, Oxford University Press, 1993.

Aristotle, *The Nicomachean Ethics*, tr. W.D. Ross, Oxford, Oxford University Press, 1954.

Attfield, Robin, *The Ethics of Environmental Concern*, 2nd edn, Athens, University of Georgia Press, 1991.

Barry, Brian and Sikora, R.I. (eds), *Obligations to Future Generations*, Philadelphia, Temple University Press, 1978.

Beauchamp, Tom L., *Case Studies in Business, Society and Ethics*, 2nd edn, Englewood Cliffs, Prentice Hall, 1989.

Beauchamp, Tom L. and Bowie, Norman E. (eds), *Ethical Theory and Business*, Englewood Cliffs, Prentice Hall, 1983.

Benedict, Ruth, 'A defense of moral relativism', in Christina Sommers and Fred Sommers (eds), *Vice and Virtue in Everyday Life*, San Diego, Harcourt Brace Jovanovich, 1989.

Blum, Lawrence, 'Compassion', in Amelie O. Rorty (ed.), *Explaining Emotions*, Berkeley, University of California Press, 1980.

Boatright, Joan, 'Aristotle meets Wall Street: the case for virtue ethics in business', *Business Ethics Quarterly*, 5 (1995), pp. 353–9.

Bok, Sissela, *Lying*, Hassocks, Harvester, 1978.

Bowie, Norman, *Business Ethics*, Englewood Cliffs, Prentice Hall, 1982.

Braybrooke, David, *Ethics and the World of Business*, Totowa, NJ, Rowman & Allanheld, 1983.

Carmichael, Sheena and Drummond, John, *Good Business*, London, Hutchinson Business Books, 1989.

Carr, Albert Z., 'Is business bluffing ethical?', in Tom L. Beauchamp and Norman E. Bowie (eds), *Ethical Theory and Business*, Englewood Cliffs, Prentice Hall, 1983 (originally published in *Harvard Business Review*, 1968).

Cederblom, Jerry and Dougherty, Charles J., *Ethics at Work*, Belmont, Wadsworth, 1990.

Chadwick, Ruth F. (ed.), *Ethics and the Professions*, Aldershot, Avebury, 1994.

Conry, Edward J., 'A critique of social contracts for business', *Business Ethics Quarterly*, 5 (1995), pp. 187–212.

Coope, Christopher Miles, 'Justice and jobs: three sceptical thoughts about rights in employment', *Journal of Applied Philosophy*, 11 (1994), pp. 71–7.

Coplon, Jeff, 'When did Johns-Manville know?', in Thomas Donaldson and Patricia H. Werhane (eds), *Ethical Issues in Business*, Englewood Cliffs, Prentice Hall, 1988.

Cordner, Christopher, 'Aristotelian virtue and its limitations', *Philosophy*, 69 (1994), pp. 291–316.

Cuilla, Joanne, 'Business ethics as moral imagination', in R. Edward Freeman (ed.), *Business Ethics*, New York, Oxford University Press, 1991.

Dees, J. Gregory and Cramton, Peter C., 'Deception and mutual trust: a reply to Strudler', *Business Ethics Quarterly*, 5 (1995), pp. 823–32.

Denyer, Nicholas, 'Chess and life: the structure of a moral code', *Aristotelian Society Proceedings*, 82 (1982), pp. 59–68.

Donaldson, Thomas, *The Ethics of International Business*, New York, Oxford University Press, 1989.

Donaldson, Thomas and Werhane, Patricia H. (eds), *Ethical Issues in Business*, Englewood Cliffs, Prentice Hall, 1988.

Emmet, D., *Rules, Roles and Relations*, London, Macmillan, 1966.

Ewin, R.E., *Co-operation and Human Values*, Brighton, Harvester, 1981.

—— 'The virtues appropriate to business', *Business Ethics Quarterly*, 5 (1995), pp. 833–42.

Foot, Philippa, 'Goodness and choice', *Aristotelian Society Supplement*, xxxv (1961).

—— 'Moral realism and moral dilemmas', *Journal of Philosophy*, 80 (1983), pp. 379–98 (reprinted in Christopher Gowans (ed.), *Moral Dilemmas*, New York, Oxford University Press).

—— (ed.) *Theories of Ethics*, Oxford, Oxford University Press, 1967.

—— The problem of abortion and the doctrine of double effect, *Oxford Review*, no. 5 (1967) (reprinted in *Virtues and Vices*, Oxford, Blackwell, 1978, pp. 19–32).

—— *Virtues and Vices*, Oxford, Blackwell, 1978.

Frankl, Viktor, *Man's Search for Meaning: an introduction to logotherapy*, tr. Ilse Lasch, London, Hodder and Stoughton, 1964.

Freeman, R. Edward (ed.), *Business Ethics*, New York, Oxford University Press, 1991.

—— *Strategic Management: a stakeholder approach*, Boston, Pitman, 1984.

Fried, Charles, *Right and Wrong*, Cambridge, Harvard University Press, 1978 (the excerpt entitled 'The evil of lying' reprinted in Christina Sommers and Fred Sommers (eds), *Vice and Virtue in Everyday Life*, San Diego, Harcourt Brace Jovanovich, 1989).

Galbraith, John Kenneth, *The Affluent Society*, 3rd edn, Boston, Houghton Mifflin, 1976.

Gauthier, David, 'Why contractarianism?', in Peter Singer (ed.), *Ethics*, Oxford, Oxford University Press, 1994.

Geach, P.T., 'Good and evil', *Analysis*, 17 (1956) (reprinted in Philippa Foot (ed.), *Theories of Ethics*, Oxford, Oxford University Press, 1967, pp. 64–73).

—— *The Virtues*, Cambridge, Cambridge University Press, 1977.

Gini, A.R., 'Case study – Manville: the ethics of economic efficiency?', in Thomas Donaldson and Patricia H. Werhane (eds), *Ethical Issues in Business*, Englewood Cliffs, Prentice Hall, 1988.

Gowans, Christopher (ed.), *Moral Dilemmas*, New York, Oxford University Press, 1987.

Graham, Pauline, 'The registrar in the John Lewis Partnership: a lesson in loyalty', *Business Ethics: A European Review*, 1 (1992), pp. 185–91.

Hamel, G., Doz, Y. and Prahalad, C.K., 'Collaborate with your competitors – and win', *Harvard Business Review*, 67 (1989), pp. 133–9.

Hampshire, Stuart, *Innocence and Experience*, Harmondsworth, Penguin, 1989.

Hampton, J., *Hobbes and the Social Contract Tradition*, Cambridge, Cambridge University Press, 1986.

Hanfling, Oswald (ed.), *The Quest for Meaning*, London, Hodder and Stoughton, 1987.

Hare, R.M., 'Geach: good and evil', *Analysis*, 18 (1957), pp. 103–12 (reprinted in Philippa Foot (ed.), *Theories of Ethics*, Oxford, Oxford University Press, 1967).

—— *Moral Thinking*, Oxford, Clarendon Press, 1981.

Harris, Nigel G.E., 'Professional codes and Kantian duties', in Ruth F. Chadwick (ed.), *Ethics and the Professions*, Aldershot, Avebury, 1994, pp. 104–15.

Hart, H.L.A., *The Concept of Law*, Oxford, Oxford University Press, 1961.

Hayek, F.A. von, 'The non sequitur of the "dependence effect"', in Tom

L. Beauchamp and Norman E. Bowie (eds), *Ethical Theory and Business*, Englewood Cliffs, Prentice Hall, 1983 (reprinted from *Southern Economic Journal*, April 1961).

Hobbes, Thomas, *Leviathan*, Oxford, Clarendon Press, 1909 (reprinted from 1651 edn).

Hosmer, La Rue Tone, *The Ethics of Management*, Boston, Irwin, 1991.

Hospers, John, 'The problem with relativism', in Christina Sommers and Fred Sommers (eds), *Vice and Virtue in Everyday Life*, San Diego, Harcourt Brace Jovanovich, 1989.

Hume, David, *A Treatise of Human Nature*, ed. L.A. Selby-Bigge, Oxford, Clarendon Press, 1888 (originally published in 1739).

—— *Enquiry Concerning the Principles of Morals*, ed. L.A. Selby-Bigge, 2nd edn, Oxford, Clarendon Press, 1902 (originally published in 1751).

Jackall, Robert, *Moral Mazes*, New York, Oxford University Press, 1988.

Jackson, Jennifer, 'Coming to ethical terms: good and bad', *Business Ethics: A European Review*, 1 (1992), pp. 211–12.

—— 'Coming to ethical terms: motive and morality', *Business Ethics: A European Review*, 1 (1992), pp. 264–6.

—— 'Coming to ethical terms: right and wrong', *Business Ethics: A European Review*, 1 (1992), 154–6.

—— 'Common codes: divergent practices', in Ruth F. Chadwick (ed.), *Ethics and the Professions*, Aldershot, Avebury, 1994, pp. 116–24.

—— 'Honesty in marketing', *Journal of Applied Philosophy*, 7 (1990), pp. 51–60.

—— 'Preserving trust in a pluralist culture', in Jack Mahoney and Elizabeth Vallance (eds), *Business Ethics in a New Europe*, Dordrecht, Kluwer, 1992, pp. 29–38.

—— 'Reconciling business imperatives and moral virtues', in Brenda Almond (ed.), *Introducing Applied Ethics*, Oxford, Blackwell, 1994, pp. 104–17.

Keeley, Michael, 'Continuing the social contract tradition', *Business Ethics Quarterly*, 5 (1995), pp. 241–55.

Kymlicka, Will, 'The social contract tradition', in Peter Singer (ed.), *A Companion to Ethics*, Oxford, Blackwell, 1993.

MacIntyre, Alasdair, *After Virtue*, 2nd edn, Indiana, University of Notre-Dame Press, 1984.

Macklin, Ruth, 'Conflicts of interest', in Tom L. Beauchamp and Norman E. Bowie (eds), *Ethical Theory and Business*, Englewood Cliffs, Prentice Hall, 1983.

Mahoney, Jack and Vallance, Elizabeth (eds), *Business Ethics in a New Europe*, Dordrecht, Kluwer, 1992.

Marx, Karl, *Capital*, London, Lawrence & Wishart, 1974 (first published in 1867).

McCracken, Janet and Shaw, Bill, 'Virtue ethics and contractarianism: towards a reconciliation', *Business Ethics Quarterly*, 5 (1995), pp. 297–312.

McElvoy, Anne, 'The moral daze', *The Spectator*, 13th January (1996), pp. 9–11.

Midgley, Mary, 'The origin of ethics', in Peter Singer (ed.), *A Companion to Ethics*, Oxford, Blackwell, 1993.

—— 'Trying out one's new sword', in Christina Sommers and Fred Sommers (eds), *Vice and Virtue in Everyday Life*, San Diego, Harcourt Brace Jovanovich, 1989.

Mill, J.S., 'Utilitarianism', in J.M. Robson, F.E.L. Priestly and D.F. Dryer (eds), *Collected Works of John Stuart Mill*, vol. X, Toronto, University of Toronto Press, 1969 (first published in 1861).

Nagel, Thomas, 'Ruthlessness in public life', in Stuart Hampshire (ed.), *Public and Private Morality*, Cambridge, Cambridge University Press, 1979.

Nash, Laura, *Good Intentions Aside*, Boston, Harvard Business School Press, 1990.

Nesteruk, Jeffrey, 'Law and the virtues: developing a legal theory for business ethics', *Business Ethics Quarterly*, 5 (1995), pp. 361–9.

Nuttall, John, *Moral Questions*, Oxford, Polity, 1993.

O'Neill, Onora, *Constructions of Reason*, Cambridge, Cambridge University Press, 1989.

Pappworth, M.H., *Human Guinea Pigs*, London, Routledge & Kegan Paul, 1967.

Partridge, Ernest (ed.), *Responsibilities to Future Generations*, New York, Prometheus Books, 1981.

Plato, *Gorgias*, tr. Walter Hamilton, Harmondsworth, Penguin, 1960.

—— 'Phaedo', in *Last Days of Socrates*, 2nd edn, tr. Hugh Tredennick, Harmondsworth, Penguin, 1959.

—— *Republic*, tr. Robin Waterfield, Oxford, Oxford University Press, 1993.

Rachels, James, 'Egoism and moral scepticism', in Christina Sommers and Fred Sommers (eds), *Vice and Virtue in Everyday Life*, San Diego, Harcourt Brace Jovanovich, 1989.

—— 'Kant and the categorical imperative', in Christina Sommers and Fred Sommers (eds), *Vice and Virtue in Everyday Life*, San Diego, Harcourt Brace Jovanovich, 1989.

Rawls, John, *A Theory of Justice*, Harvard, Harvard University Press, 1971.

Robson, J.M., Priestly, F.E.L. and Dryer, D.F. (eds), *Collected Works of John Stuart Mill*, Toronto, University of Toronto Press, 1969.

Rorty, Amelie O. (ed.), *Explaining Emotions*, Berkeley, University of California Press, 1980.

Russell, Bertrand, *A History of Western Philosophy*, London, George Allen and Unwin, 1946.

Selwyn, Norman M., *Laws of Employment*, 8th edn, London, Butterworths, 1993.

Seth, Vikram, *A Suitable Boy*, London, Phoenix House, 1993.

Sieff, Marcus, *Management the Marks & Spencer Way*, London, Fontana/Collins, 1990.

Shaw, Bill, 'Virtues for a postmodern world', *Business Ethics Quarterly*, 5 (1995), pp. 843–63.

Singer, Peter (ed.), *A Companion to Ethics*, Oxford, Blackwell, 1993.

—— (ed.) *Ethics*, Oxford, Oxford University Press, 1994.

—— *How Are We to Live?*, London, Mandarin, 1994.

—— 'Why act morally?', in Christina Sommers and Fred Sommers (eds), *Vice and Virtue in Everyday Life*, San Diego, Harcourt Brace Jovanovich, 1989.

Slote, Michael, *Goods and Virtues*, Oxford, Clarendon Press, 1983.

Smart, J.J.C. and Williams, Bernard, *Utilitarianism For and Against*, Cambridge, Cambridge University Press, 1973.

Solomon, Robert C., 'Business ethics', in Peter Singer (ed.), *A Companion to Ethics*, Oxford, Blackwell, 1993.

—— *Ethics and Excellence*, New York, Oxford University Press, 1992.

Sommers, Christina and Sommers, Fred (eds), *Vice and Virtue in Everyday Life*, San Diego, Harcourt Brace Jovanovich, 1989.

Sorell, Tom and Hendry, John, *Business Ethics*, Oxford, Butterworth–Heinemann, 1994.

Stace, Walter T., 'Ethical relativity and ethical absolutism', in Thomas Donaldson and Patricia H. Werhane (eds), *Ethical Issues in Business*, Englewood Cliffs, Prentice Hall, 1988.

Sternberg, Elaine, *Just Business*, London, Little, Brown, 1994.

—— 'Teleology and business ethics', in Wojceich W. Gasparksi and Leo Ryan (eds), *Human Action in Business: praxiological and ethical dimensions*, vol. 5, *Praxiology*, New York, Rutgers University Press, 1996.

Strudler, Alan, 'On the ethics of deception in negotiation', *Business Ethics Quarterly*, 5 (1995), pp. 805–22.

Sumner, William Graham, 'A defense of cultural relativism', in Thomas Donaldson and Patricia H. Werhane (eds), *Ethical Issues in Business*, Englewood Cliffs, Prentice Hall, 1988.

Tamari, Meir, *In the Marketplace*, Southfield, Targum Press, 1991.

Thucydides, *History of the Peloponnesian War*, Loeb edition, vol. 3, tr. Charles Forster Smith, London, William Heinemann, 1921.

Vallance, Elizabeth, *Business Ethics at Work*, Cambridge, Cambridge University Press, 1995.

Velasquez, Manuel, 'International business ethics: the aluminium companies in Jamaica', *Business Ethics Quarterly*, 5 (1995), pp. 865–82.

Wallace, James D., *Virtues and Vices*, Ithaca, Cornell University Press, 1978.

Warnock, G.J., *The Object of Morality*, London, Methuen, 1971.

Weil, Simone, *Seventy Letters*, tr. Richard Rees, London, Oxford University Press, 1965.

Williams, Bernard, *Morality*, Cambridge, Cambridge University Press, 1976 (originally published by Harper & Row, 1972).

—— 'Politics and moral character', in *Moral Luck*, Cambridge, Cambridge University Press, 1981.

Winkler, Earl R. and Coombs, Jerrold R., *Applied Ethics: a reader*, Cambridge, MA, Blackwell, 1993.

Wong, David, 'Relativism', in Peter Singer (ed.), *A Companion to Ethics*, Oxford, Blackwell, 1993.

Index